THE PRACTICAL
WOOD TURNER

" Tools do what *you* want them to do
when you know what *they* want to do "

MY INSTRUCTIONS MEAN JUST WHAT THEY SAY.
You may be troubled with tools digging in. Well, if you follow my words carefully, they won't. My aim is to show you how to cut wood as it prefers to be cut.

The Practical Wood Turner

Use of Gouge and Chisel
Face-Plate Turning
Chucking: Parting: Boring
Special Work, Etc.

F. Pain

DRAKE PUBLISHERS INC   NEW YORK
381 Park Avenue South
New York, N.Y. 10016

Published in 1974 by
Drake Publishers Inc.
381 Park Avenue South
New York, New York 10016

ISBN 0-87749-705-2
LCCCN 74-6436

Printed in the United States of America

CONTENTS

INTRODUCTION

THE Worshipful Company of Turners once bought a trumpet for six shillings to blow at their dinners. I am hoping to provide you with a sort of feast on wood-turning, and so please allow me a modest blow on my trumpet first. The aim of this book is to set you thinking on the right lines, so that you *cut wood as it prefers to be cut.* It would be easy to give bare instructions and designs, but it is much better when you know why we do a job in a certain way. It enables you to apply the idea to your own work.

I have been associated with wood-turning for fifty years and have had a business of my own, doing furniture work both antique and modern, builders' requirements up to some fifteen feet long, fancy wood-ware for gift shops, automatic lathe work, and extremely accurate work for instruments. During the last five years or so I have been to exhibitions and schools demonstrating and answering questions, and I've been to a prison too.

Now this fanfare on my trumpet is blown solely to give you confidence that it is a practical man who is trying to help you with advice. I say this in all sincerity. The best way to learn a trade is to compete in quality and price with others, and so I'll now retire and get on with the job until I hear Gabriel blowing *his* trumpet.

Now, whereas you can *scrape* an object to shape without any trouble, good wood-turning runs very close indeed to spoiling the work. If, however, you follow my instructions carefully, you should be able to learn just how it is done. Remember that scraping is not true craftsmanship at all. Should you be like one man I know who throws the job he is doing across the shop if it is difficult, well, throw the tools as well. You see, I get disheartened when I hear a man say, "Oh! he's a blooming expert, I can't do it." Believe me, many "blinking amateurs" do far better work than some "blooming experts". So go forward and enjoy wood-turning, one of those creative arts still left to us, and create things with your own personality written in wood.

My instructions mean just what they say. For instance, they advise you to hold the tools lightly. At exhibitions I often swank, and although I use all the power the motor will give yet hold the tool lightly between two fingers only. You may be troubled with tools digging in. Well, if you follow the words carefully, they won't.

It would be much better to show you personally how to use the tools, but I cannot reach everybody and have therefore to rely on words and sketches.

It would be nice to see the book propped up in front of the lathe, and a scrap piece of wood in the lathe and you trying out the movements (quite a lot would prefer to learn boxing this way). My five years of demonstrating have taught me a lot of what people wish to know. Generally I prefer to teach boys and ladies because they both do what they are told (?), at least when turning. Men will invariably force the tools around, although, believe me, the tools will do the jobs themselves if you only hold them right.

You will find ideas for turning everywhere around you; such things as railings often have nice finishes on them; the jewellers will have some nice shapes for cruet sets or light candlesticks; the antique shops often have some old things which suggest items to make. My men used to say that I saw too much. Once a chalk mark and date was put on the factory wall. It puzzled me, so I asked what it was for. It seems that I remarked that a certain job was perfect, and, as I had done many hundreds of pounds' worth of work for the King's woodcarver, it must have pleased me. Well, constructive criticism always helps, especially when you apply it to your own work.

F. PAIN.

High Wycombe,
1956.

Since I wrote this book in 1956, I've travelled a great deal, demonstrating, and wish to thank many for their kindness. Little did I know when I started that it would mean so much travelling. This year, 1965, I've my fourth car.

I once listened to some profound words on education at a teachers' refresher course at Durham, and I replied—

"Many children who cannot express themselves in other ways such as music or mathematics can excel in wood turning; in fact some who might be called idiots are extremely good with their hands, and that is why I'm so good at it."

Anyway I do put forward wood turning as a rewarding hobby. Cutting wood as it prefers to be cut is the aim of this book. Just stop the lathe and hold the tool on the work as I say in the following pages, and in nearly all cases you will see that it has a *paring action*, and this is the ideal to strive for. You do wood turning by *feel* as much as sight, and that is why even blind people can do it.

High Wycombe, 1965   F. PAIN.

THE PRACTICAL
WOOD TURNER

CHAPTER I : ABOUT LATHES

MACHINERY is often made locally to suit a trade, and a consultation between maker and user results in something that really suits the user. First was the bodger's lathe which revolved back and forth, being pulled in the return stroke by the branch of a tree. This gradually gave way to the wheel lathe which often needed

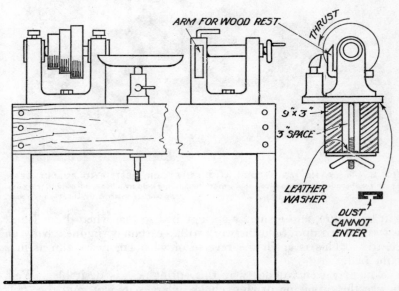

FIG. I. WOOD BED LATHE OF TYPE WIDELY USED IN THE TRADE
The bed is made of B.C. pine bolted to uprights. This drawing is diagrammatic and is intended to show the main lay-out, not to give details.

help in treadling, especially when turning a big job. Then steam came along, and so we had power lathes—one firm made them by hundreds for the local furniture firms. The factory where I worked as a boy had fourteen of them, and they did over six thousand designs of furniture. Electricity succeeded steam, and firms began to make lathes who had not this link with a local trade to tell them just what was wanted. Thus it is we now have many lathes which are not as suitable for wood-turning as they could be. So many manufacturers think in terms of metal-turning lathes and design our wood-turning lathes accordingly.

Wood bed lathe. The standard practice locally in my time was to cast the headstock with two lugs $1\frac{1}{2}$ in. wide. The lathe bed had a 3-in. space between its beds, so you can see how loose the fit was. Engineers' lathes would be hopeless with such a lot of play, but it was no disadvantage to us. The lathe bed consisted of two pieces of 9-in. by 3-in. British Columbian pine as shown in Fig. 1. This is

FIG. 2. 6-in. LATHE HEADSTOCK AND TAILSTOCK, REST, AND PULLEY GEAR.
These are intended to be mounted on a timber bed, being held by a heavy screw and wing nut.
By courtesy Dexter & Co. Ltd., High Wycombe.

soft by nature, and formed a springy bed so that when the tailstock was tightened up it held the work with a certain springiness between centres. This is again the reverse of what engineers aim at in a lathe bed.

You may well wonder why this springiness is desirable. Well, in use the prong or driving chuck enlarges its slot, and the tail-stock centre bores a little into the other end. The springiness takes this up so that we don't have to be continually tightening up the tail-stock wheel. In this way the metal bed and small centre height of the modern lathe go against us.

And here let me say that some great engineers have made the mistake of thinking that solidity is needed, whereas it is really springiness that is wanted. Isambard Kingdom Brunel was a great engineer (1806–1859) who thought that railway lines ought to be on

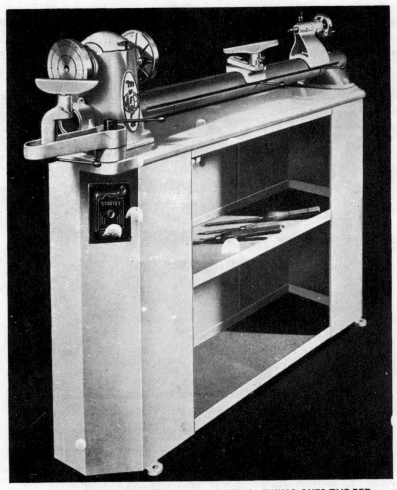

FIG. 3.   THE M.L.8 MOTORISED LATHE WITH 8-in. SWING OVER THE BED.
Standard distance between centres is 30 in.   Longer bed lengths are available.   Large diameter work, bowls, etc. can be turned on a face plate at the other side of the headstock as
shown.   The lathe is also available without the stand.
By courtesy Myford Engineering Co. Ltd., Nottingham.

a very solid foundation, and so laid large baulks of timber lengthwise along the track bolted to stakes driven into the earth.   In the
event this proved too solid in use, and the track is laid on sleepers
to-day in the way you well know.   Have you noticed how the
sleepers allow the rail to go up and down as the train goes over them?

Thus it is that I prefer a lathe with a wood bed and a fine solid head with solid bearings to a light lathe with a host of attachments such as steadies, etc., that we cannot use. On the other hand I do realize that the space occupied is important to the man who has only

FIG. 4. THE CORONET MAJOR LATHE WITH 4½-in. CLEARANCE BETWEEN CENTRE AND BED.
For turning large diameter work the headstock can be pivoted round at right angles to the bed, enabling table tops, etc. to be turned.

By courtesy Coronet Tool Co., Derby.

a small workshop, and the all-metal lathe is capable of good work (it must be or the firms making them would go bankrupt).

Bearings. Ball bearings seem ideal as the thrust is rather heavy on a wood-turning lathe, because, owing to the poor centres often fitted, we often have to force them (more anon about these). One trade lathe I know has bearings $4\frac{1}{4}$ in. long by 2 in. diameter, but of course it would use a lot of power (what a lovely solid job for face-turning it would be). So perhaps ball bearings are all right as we have so little power to play with as a rule. Furthermore if the oil can is not used freely a plain bearing would soon be ruined. In any case we cannot use the large single-phase motor that solid bearings would need from the house supply. As for speed, why waste power unnecessarily? 1,400 r.p.m. is ample in the lathes we have in mind.

The power that a lathe consumes is a very real problem, but we should grumble more if it were missing. For face-turning I could easily use all a 2-h.p. motor could give (a 5-h.p. was fitted to mine). It is usual to fit a 1-h.p. motor for spindle work, which is much lighter on the power consumed.

Centres. In our trade our centres screw in and need no hole right through the headstock to poke them out, as there is a hole across by which they may be unscrewed with a tommy-bar. Taper

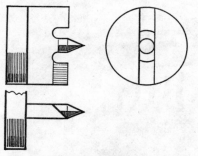

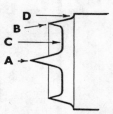

FIG. 5. CORRECT FORM OF FORK CHUCK.
Note that edges of prongs are staggered.

FIG. 6. RING TAIL-STOCK CENTRE.
A. Centre point. B. Ring. C. Flat. D. Shoulder. Both C and D should push against end of wood.

centres often get fixed in, and force has to be used to poke them out—which does the ball races no good.

Just what steel some driving centres are made of is a mystery to me. The prongs bend over inwardly, and it is not good enough. The tail-stock centre pushes only, and ordinary bright bolts turned suitably have proved to be all right, so long as we don't knock our wood sideways between centres to true it. Manufactured centres, however, should stand up to this, as it is the accepted way of turning squares. Fig. 5 shows how a centre should look. Some centres have no space between centre point and fangs, and so long as nothing prevents the fangs from penetrating into the end grain all is well. You could file this away, and also touch up the bevel, which is 45° and flat on the driving side.

In the trade we never stop our lathes in spindle work but put our hand around the wood and ease back the tail-stock. Someone once asked my man if the wood often hits you, and he assured him, "No, generally only once." Still I would not advise you if I thought it dangerous practice, and if your hand is around the work all is well. The reason for not stopping the power is that small A/C motors don't like being started and stopped. If the centre does not come away easily out of the wood, look for a burr on the driving centre, as this is probably the cause. Whenever we have trouble with a tail-stock

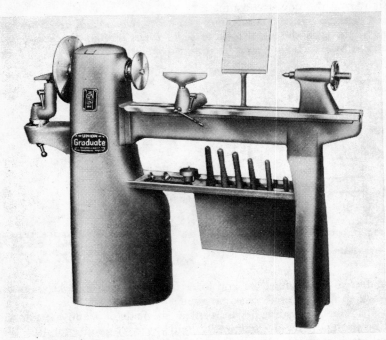

FIG. 7. GRADUATE LATHE WITH EITHER 5-in. OR 6-in. HEIGHT OF CENTRE.
"I helped to design this lathe. It is especially suitable for schools."
By courtesy T. S. Harrison & Sons Ltd., Heckmondwike.

centre burning we look at the driving centre first (but then our tail-stock centres are of the correct shape). You may be troubled with a deep groove in the tail-stock centre filling up with charcoal. Well, it should not be there.

Fig. 6 shows a correct ring centre. The flat part pushes the wood on to the driving chuck and is not very deep. The fact that a tail-stock centre pushes cannot be too strongly emphasized, for so many fail here.   With a happy pair of centres which don't need continual tightening up we shall enjoy wood-turning.

A special centre we found useful was a long one that went into the hole of a candlestick (which is always bored first).   We also had some other special sizes so that when we turned pins or dowels on the work we could make the size of the pins the same as the centre. This saved using callipers.

Rests.   Lathe rests get me all hot and cross, for some are just as awkward as they can be.   If only lathe manufacturers would draw

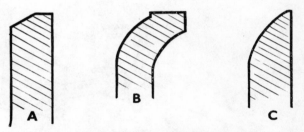

FIG. 8. SECTIONS THROUGH DIFFERENT RESTS.
"I do not like either A or B.   That at C is the best shape."

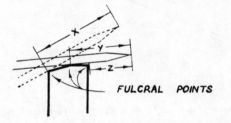

FIG. 9. "SIDE VIEW OF REST WHICH I DO NOT FAVOUR."
This shows how the tool passes through an abrupt
change as the handle is raised or lowered, owing to
its bearing upon a different point of the rest.

a curved line for the top of the rest to show its section, then show a tool with the handle moving up and down as in turning, they would make much better rests.   All sorts of things get in the way as we move the tool about, not to mention the shape of the rest itself.   A parallel rest is wanted, as we sometimes slide the hand along it.   I admit it does not look so nice as a shaped one, but we have them for use.

I know of a very cheap lathe, and one that costs £3,500.   Both have perfect rests (I shall one day) and they cost no more to make than poor ones. Some rests have fancy shaped tops, and as we do curves the tool rests on different parts just as a sort of handicap. Fig. 8 shows what I mean.

The ideal rest for spindle work is made of wood. A pin goes into the T rest and stand, and an L bolt (X) holds the other end. Fig. 10 shows clearly the idea. The idea could be worked out to suit the particular lathe. All trade lathes have this form of rest, and it is deal. They need truing up from time to time as they mark in use,

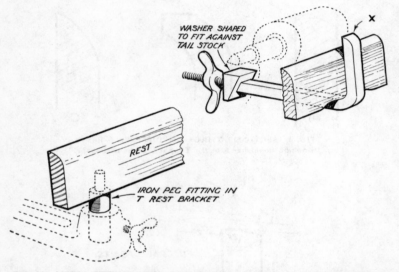

WASHER SHAPED
TO FIT AGAINST
TAIL STOCK

X

REST

IRON PEG FITTING IN
T REST BRACKET

FIG. 10. METAL FITTING USED FOR ATTACHING WOOD REST TO LATHE.

so a spokeshave is included among the tools. This marking or notching on the rest is an advantage in repetition work, however. The notches formed by the tools prevent slips and spoilt work. Another advantage is that we can have the rest the length of the work, and this saves having to move it about.

For faceplate work we do use a metal rest, and please see that it is forward enough to be near the work, as when, say, turning a bread board. A rest just above its pin is of little use, for the stand gets in the way.

Drive. Trade lathes have a countershaft with fast and loose pulleys so that the flat belt 2 in. wide can be slid gradually on. This is useful for some work, and I feel that a clutch (which might only raise the motor up) to allow a V belt to slip a bit would be an improvement. Some people might think a lathe with 7- or 8-in. centres could not do small work. Well, one lathe we had did finials for a building which had balls 16 in. in diameter; and also did a pair

FIG. 11. CORRECT HEIGHT FOR COMFORTABLE WORKING.
The centre is about in line with the elbow.

of candlesticks for "The Queen's Doll's House" which went away in a matchbox.

No part of the stand holding the lathe bed ought to be more forward than the edge of the bed itself or it will be in the way of the feet. A useful height is when the elbow with hand up is centre height as in Fig. 11. It avoids bending the back.

Now I've often said, "Listen to an expert's advice then do it your own way", and the late Mr. Middleton of garden fame said,

2—P.W.T.

"People have done exactly the opposite of what I recommend with most excellent results." I often think of expert musicians in church who so complicate the music that we cannot join in. May I very sincerely say that I want to encourage good wood-turning, and help you to enjoy it. My job is not to run down anything, but rather to set everyone thinking clearly about what is wanted.

To my simple mind to have a round bed, then to fit a saddle on to it with a flat surface on top to hold a T-rest stand seems wrong in design, for it could have been flat at the start if only a flat bed had been used. (This does not mean that lathes so fitted are wrong, as other reasons probably governed the design.) The flat top of the bed takes the downward thrust in a more straight forward way as Fig. 1 shows. There is also a lot to be said for a design that does not clog up with dust or polish. Some of us use friction polish in the lathe, and it *will* get on to the lathe bed. Still the lathes sold are capable of good work, so don't go all sorry and sad over this chapter.

FIG. 12.   MACHINE FOR TWIST TURNING SHOWING MASTER PATTERN.
It is not practicable to do twist turning in the ordinary simple lathe.   This machine has a revolving head (centre) with specially shaped cutters.   The wood is passed across this head and revolved spiralwise, being controlled by the master pattern in the tail-stock.

By courtesy of Dexter & Co., Ltd., High Wycombe.

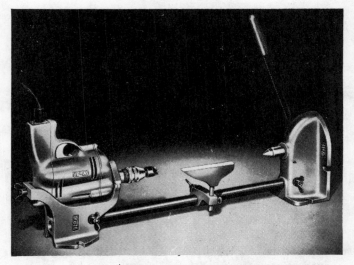

FIG. 13. WOLF CUB LATHE POWERED BY AN ELECTRIC DRILL.
For small work this gives good results. A small face plate is also available.
By courtesy Wolf Electric Tools Ltd., London.

FIG. 14. UTILITY LATHE DRIVEN BY AN ELECTRIC DRILL.
Either between-centre work or small face plate work can be done.
By courtesy Black & Decker Ltd., Harmondsworth.

"CUTTING WOOD AS IT PREFERS TO BE CUT."

One of the secrets of both gouge and chisel turning is to let the bevel of the tool rub the work. If it does this the tool cannot dig in. But don't just take my word for it. Get your tools and try it for yourself.

CHAPTER 2 : YOUR TOOLS—GOUGES

IT does seem to me that to have the right tools and to sharpen them properly is a tremendous help in wood turning. I therefore give straightway what I recommend. Fig. 1 gives the chisels and gouges used for true turning, and Fig. 4 the scraping tools for face plate work and special jobs. I show them here in a group so that you have a good idea of what is wanted, but I discuss them in detail in the chapters dealing with their use.

GOUGES

The local tool merchants in High Wycombe stock the tools in Fig. 1, for they are used in the furniture trade here, but curiously few are in the booklets issued by the British Standards Institution. I once asked a manufacturer what a certain tool was used for. He replied that he did not know, but it was easy to make. I then asked why he did not make deep half-round gouges and was told that they are hard to make.

Well this is a sorry start and things are likely to get worse because fewer wood-turning tools are being used by the trade since automatic machines do the bulk of the work. On the other hand there are many more amateur hand-turners about, men who do wood turning as a relaxation from their normal jobs. Unfortunately the amateur does not know the best shape for tools. There are far too many shallow gouges about, and I suspect that manufacturers make them because they are easy to forge.

Range of gouges. First let us consider the tools, and I turn to the gouges in my own kit (Fig. 1). I've a $\frac{3}{8}$ in., deep, long and strong (A), which I use for rough turning any size of bowl. Then I've a $\frac{3}{8}$ in., long and strong (B), but just a plain half of a circle, not a shallow one. Another useful gouge I have is a $\frac{3}{4}$-in. half-round (C), which is ample for most roughing-out purposes; also a $1\frac{1}{4}$ in. (D), the same, which youngsters enjoy to handle, but which I like for turning the larger legs, etc., used in the furniture trade. A $\frac{1}{4}$-in., rather deep gouge, long and strong (E), for deep hollows; and a $\frac{1}{4}$-in. half-round (F), for simple hollows. The only shallow type of gouge is a $\frac{5}{8}$ in. (G), which is useful for hollows in the feet of chair legs as it is practically the finished shape desired.

The caption says that these tools are used by me, but, alas, so

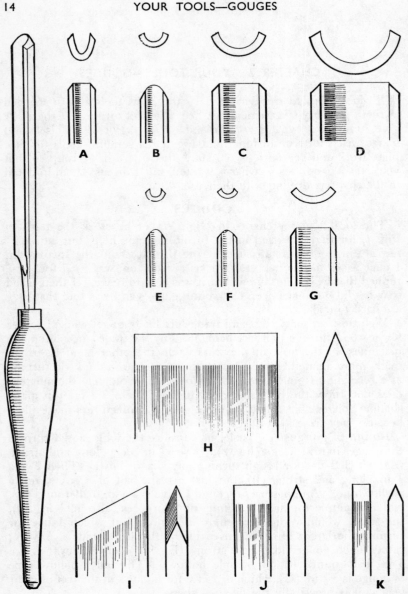

FIG. I. GOUGES AND CHISELS I USE IN TURNING.

A. ¾ in.-deep long and strong.   B. ⅜ in. half-round long and strong.   C. ½-in. half-round.
D. 1¼-in. half-round.   E. ¼-in. deep, long and strong.   F. ¼-in. half-round.   G. ⅜-in. shallow.
H. 2-in. square.   I. 1-in. long-cornered.   J. ½-in. square.   K. ¼-in. square.

many ask for my tools at demonstrations, they seldom are in my tool box for long. Few tool merchants stock them, in fact I know of only one who does. Many years ago you could buy a case containing seventy-five gouges all different, but you cannot to-day. Actually it is not necessary to have so many and I ask manufacturers for just six on your behalf.

Gouges are generally required to remove wood quickly while chisels are for paring a nice surface, but, of course, gouges are necessary to finish off hollows in turning. So let us look at gouges (C) and (D), which I suggest you grind square across as in Fig. 2. You will notice that no matter how you rotate the gouge the cutting edge is the same. Thus the whole of the cutting edge can be used.

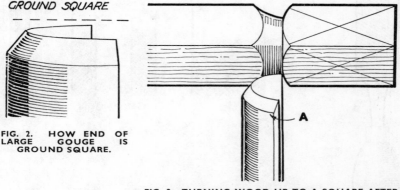

GROUND SQUARE

FIG. 2. HOW END OF LARGE GOUGE IS GROUND SQUARE.

FIG. 3. TURNING WOOD UP TO A SQUARE AFTER END OF LATTER HAS BEEN ROUNDED WITH THE CHISEL.

Some gouges are ground to a nose for another purpose, but (C) and (D) are roughing-out gouges intended to turn wood up to about 2 or $2\frac{1}{2}$ in. The larger the diameter of the work the smaller the gouge we use, generally speaking. Of course it depends on the power available (when in business I had 5 h.p.), and the kind of wood and length of work also play their parts.

Using the gouge. Fig. 3 shows, say, a 2-in. square cut down to leave a pummel or square part. The gouge is laid on its side, and I would like you to hold the gouge lightly and do that cut. Notice how bevel (A) tends to move the gouge to the right, for it naturally slides that way. The idea I'm trying to get across is that tools do the job themselves if only they are presented correctly to the job. I've amused many by holding tools very lightly to show the idea

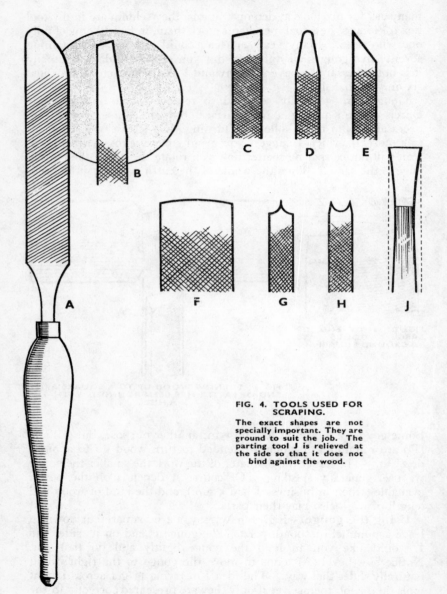

FIG. 4. TOOLS USED FOR SCRAPING.

The exact shapes are not specially important. They are ground to suit the job. The parting tool J is relieved at the side so that it does not bind against the wood.

and to try to stop people forcing them about (you could with force move the tool against its natural tendencies).

Please try out the movements now.   If you hold the tool lightly, you will get the feel of it.   If you lay the gouge over on the other side, it will tend to move to the left, and this is how I remove the wood, as in a chair leg for instance.   Any part of the cutting edge can be used between the pummels; and if you are lazy, you can even make the tool work itself along the leg by moving the handle end a little to the left, or right.   I don't know whether lazy is the right word: I find that I do it myself anyway.   Fig. 5 shows a cylinder being roughed out with the gouge.

FIG. 5.   CYLINDER WITH SQUARES AT THE ENDS BEING TURNED.
The ends of the squares are cut in with the chisel (see page 111) and the half-round gouge used between.   See also Fig. 3.

Some may ask, "What is the correct height for the rest?"   Well, just what suits you is correct so long as the bevel of the tool rubs the work.   The comfortable height of centres seems to be your elbow when your hand is on the shoulder as you stand upright (see page 9). If the lathe is too low, you may find a higher rest a help.   Many lathes are made for school use and are too low for adults.   It is easy to raise it up and is well worth making the alteration.

Many of you will have a shallow gouge, and it will take a broad shaving rather than a rope-like one.   It will tend to lift the work out of the lathe if it is a springy job, and in any case it won't remove wood so easily and will need holding more carefully.   A chisel can remove wide shavings, but a curved wide shaving has considerable strength.

ROUGHING DOWN WITH THE LARGE GOUGE.
I always grind this gouge square with no point or nose (see D, Fig. I, page 14). This
enables every part of the edge to be used since it can be rotated.

It will force the tool down whereas a flat shaving just bends.   So these shallow gouges tend to dig in if used for heavy cuts.

You may understand better about curved shavings by thinking of those flexible steel rules that will stand straight out because they are curved in section.   That is the reason why for springy work or large diameter work we use a smaller size of gouge.   The shallow wide gouges are used for hand-turned brush handles and of course cannot turn a hollow smaller than their own radius.   A small radius gouge used for the same job could show ribs.

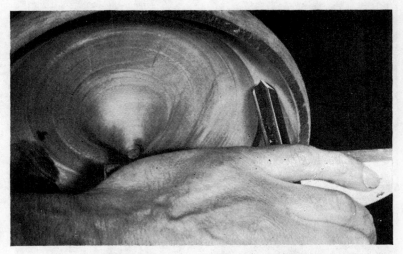

FIG. 6.   TURNING THE INSIDE OF A BOWL WITH THE GOUGE.
The end of the gouge is ground square (A, Fig. I, page 14), and the bevel at about 45°
The bevel must rub the whole time.
By courtesy E. Barrs, Myford Engineering Co. Ltd.

Gouges are made *ordinary* and *long and strong* (often labelled L and S only).   It is the section of these roughing-out gouges that gives them their strength.   The ordinary kind is all right for normal work.   The L and S would be used for large diameter table legs because the cutting edge may have to project a long way from the rest when turning hollows.

L and S gouge.   Let us have a look at (A) Fig. 1, which is a ³⁄₈-in. deep L and S, a favourite of mine for bowl turning.   (E) is the same but smaller and would be ideal for hardwood, say, turning oak bowls from some old church timber.   (A) is ground square across when used for bowl turning or face plate work, and if I could write in three dimensions I could show why more easily.   However,

I will try by a photograph.   Fig. 6 shows the tool well inside a bowl, and you can see that if the gouge were ground to a nose it would not take the heavy cut the turner is taking.   It would be ground away just where it is wanted, for the side of gouge is cutting and the bevel at the centre is resting on the wood.

This bevel resting on the work prevents that dig-in which worries so many people.   The handle end of the tool is held well down,

FIG. 7. GOUGE IS TURNED OVER ON SIDE WHEN TURNING OUTSIDE OF BOWL.
Note how bevel rubs. Compare with Fig. 8.

and so presents the cutting edge at a favourable angle to cut.   Note, however, that the gouge is ground at at least 45°.   Any lower angle than this will cause digging in because the bevel will be unable to rub on the wood owing to the angle at which it must be presented. I am grateful for permission to use this photograph as it is the best I've seen to show this principle.

Fig. 7 shows me holding the gouge on the outside of a bowl, and Fig. 8 illustrates the complete movement.   Quite frequently, however, it is the side of the gouge rather than its middle that does

most of the work.   That is the reason I like a deep L and S gouge
for this kind of work; the large diameter can be a strain on the tool.
Fig. 8 shows how the movement of the handle end of the gouge
governs the shape of the work.   You can try this principle on both
inside and outside of the bowl.   Perhaps you can see that if you
move the gouge from A to B it cuts deeper into the wood, and so we
vary the shape by this movement.   A correctly ground tool tends

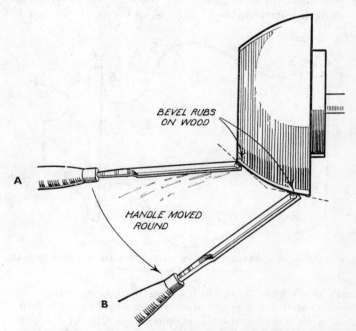

FIG. 8.   PLAN VIEW SHOWING OUTSIDE OF BOWL BEING TURNED.
Note how the handle is swung round to enable the bevel to follow the curve.

to keep against the wood by the action of its shaving, and would dig
in bodily if the bevel did not rub and so prevent it.

Letting the bevel rub.   To learn more about this tool try to
turn the wood without the bevel rubbing the work and let the centre
of the tool cut.   It may dig in or shudder and you can only maintain
an even cut by using force.   This is the very thing I wish you to
avoid, for it is impossible to feel the tool working if you hold it
tightly.   When I'm swanking I just hold the end of the tool handle
between two fingers and take off heavy cuts, even slowing up the

motor. The rope-like shavings run down the hollow of the gouge which shows that you are *cutting wood as it prefers to be cut.*

My swanking demonstrations are to give you confidence in turning, as those who can feel the tool working get so much pleasure from it. A blind man I taught does it for a living now, and says that he enjoys it so much that he will turn in his grave. If I can show you how to get such pleasure, I shall be indeed humbly grateful.

Bevel of tool. The bevels of my tools are shorter than many people think is correct. Well, there is no correct bevel but if too

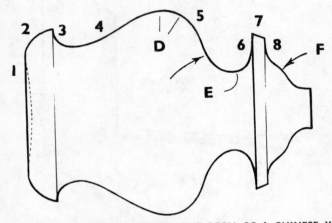

FIG. 9. DESIGN FOR TABLE LAMP IN THE FORM OF A CHINESE VASE.
It measures about 5 in. in diameter.

long they don't seem to retain for long their sharpness. Furthermore you cannot use a gouge with a long bevel inside a bowl. A friend of mine who has the "Freedom of the City of London" for his hand-turning seems to use the bevels that I do and so do tradesmen generally, so it is probably right, but by all means try out other bevels. (B) and (F), Fig. 1, could have a longer bevel and be ground to a nose rather than square across, for they are for turning hollows. If a gouge is rather wide for the hollow we wish to turn, it is ground more pointed.

Ming vase table lamp. Now if you break the minute hand off the clock and put it in front of you and fix a nice chunk of wood in the lathe, we will try to follow what a gouge can do. The Westminster Abbey clock would do as that has only an hour hand, but it will help to follow how to twist the gouge in turning shapes. Fig. 10 shows the idea. The gouge is how you would see it when

using it—that is, you are standing behind it with the handle next
to you.   The clock times given refer only to how the gouge is twisted,
not to other movements such as the handle end up or down and
sideways.   We will use the ⅜-in. half-round L and S gouge only, but
any gouge you have will work the same in principle, so don't hold
up the job because you have not one (very few people have).

There are two ways of rounding our square, one by moving it
along the rest, which is the usual way of doing it; but for some
unknown reason I prefer to tilt the gouge to 2 o'clock with handle
well to right, and keep lifting the handle.   It may well be owing to
the fact that many lathes I work won't swing a large block and I have
to start with the T rest stand at the end of the work.   So now we have
a round block of wood, and you can try out the movements which
refer to the final cut rather than those just removing wood.   Fig. 9
shows the shape to be turned.

Detail No. 2 is done with the gouge at 12 o'clock *always starting at*

FIG. 10. DIAGRAM SHOWING GOUGE POSITION AS SEEN BY USER.

the largest diameter.   Then, twisting the gouge to 9.30 as you move
handle to right, gradually lift it, which of course moves the cutting
edge downwards.   The centre of the gouge does the cutting and
bevel underneath rubs the work.   For a larger curve than that
shown the gouge could slide along the rest to the left slightly; in
fact quite large balls can be turned this way.   I suggest that you refer
to these movements in what you wish to do, rather than copy the
whole design (unless you wish to, of course).

Detail 3 is started with gouge at 1 o'clock and handle to right.
When in a little way the gouge is twisted to 2.30 and the handle
moved over to the right so that the bevel is square to the work.   We
would like to start with the gouge at 2.30 and the bevel square to the
centre line of the work, but until we were in a little way the bevel
could not rub and the gouge might slip into the wood and spoil
the shape.   But you could try holding the tool more firmly just
for the start and see whether you manage starting the curve at 2.30
rather than 1 o'clock.

You will notice if we use a gouge with too obtuse an angle for the
bevel we have to move the handle too far over, and that is why we

use different angles for gouges used in spindle turning than for face plate work. We gradually lift the handle and twist the gouge to 12 as we move the handle to left. For an inside curve as that shown the tool does not slide along the rest, but ends square to the work and at 12 o'clock, but for larger curves it could slide to the right a bit so that it ends as above.

Detail 4 is done with the gouge at 2, sliding it along the rest as we lift the handle. It is a case of sliding it and lifting handle in 2 co-ordinated movement to follow the desired outline. A chisel would be better, but more skill is required on large diameter stuff, and this is a safer way of doing it. The gouge is square to work, that is handle neither to left or right and you could twist the gouge to 12 o'clock at bottom of hollow but that's not important in long hollows. Detail 5 starts with gouge at 12 o'clock, gradually twisting it to 2.15 and sliding it along the rest to right a little.

PARTING
TOOL

FIG. II. PARTING TOOL
USED EACH SIDE OF
LIP PROJECTION.

This brings us to the arrow. You may note that so far it is just the same as detail 2 only larger and the other way round. The tool is twisted gradually to 12 o'clock as we lift the handle, and the cut ends at the bottom of hollow. You will notice that just twisting the gouge from 2.15 to 12 o'clock makes the tool do the shape itself; the bevel pushes it round the curve, so to speak.

Cutting detail 6 and 8 could slip and remove 7 entirely for until we have a surface to rest the bevel of the gouge on it has no support, so if you fear that you will slip up just push in a parting tool or $\frac{1}{4}$-in.

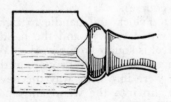

FIG. 12. OGEE FINISH TO PUMMEL.

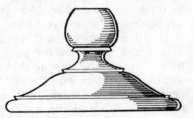

FIG. 13. OGEE SHAPE TO BASE OF
STANDARD.

chisel as in Fig. 11. The bevel of the tool will then rest against the surface. Only go a short way in for the cuts will not leave a clean cut surface Detail 7 removes the roughness later. If you do this detail note that 6 starts at 9.30, and detail 8 at 2.30. If you do not use the parting tool, detail 6 starts with the gouge at 11 and the handle to the left. Gradually twist the handle to 9.30 and lift the handle, then twist the tool to the end at 12 at the bottom of the hollow. This is similar to detail 3 but the other way round.

Detail 8 is started with the handle to the right and gouge at 1.

FIG. 14. TURNING NECK OF MING VASE.
The gouge is taken in from the larger to the smaller diameter, and the bevel rubs the whole time.

Roll the gouge over to 2.30 and move the handle more to the right so that the bevel is square to the centre line of the work. Lift the handle too, at the same time, bringing us to arrow (F). We must now move the handle to the left a little which will move the tool more to the right because of the bevel rubbing the work. The rest acts as a fulcrum and we twist the tool to 1.30, moving the handle to the left a little more and gradually twisting the gouge to 2.30.

Now we slide the tool along the rest to the right, and, as we lift

3—P.W.T.

the handle more we twist the gouge to 12.30.   This makes the tool
do a nice hollow all by itself; you only move and twist the tool.
This rather involved procedure might be better followed if you think
of the point of the gouge doing the work and twist it accordingly.
A similar shape is often used on table legs and table lamps as in
Figs. 12 and 13, so it is a process well worth learning.

Detail 7 is simple.   With gouge at 1.30 we move the handle to
the left which shifts the cutting edge to the right.   It does not slide

FIG. 15. HOW "LID" OF VASE IS TURNED WITH GOUGE.
As before, work from the larger to the smaller diameter.

along the rest, but only swivels, and, as we do it, we lift the handle
a little.   For detail 1 the tool is held at 10 with the handle well to
left so that the bevel is practically at right angles with the work.
You just lift the handle, and when you hear the chuck being turned
as well you have gone too far.   To make a nice clean bottom reverse
the wood in the chuck and do it with point of the long-cornered
chisel.   It may be of interest to know that something like this design
is in the British Museum and is Chinese of the Ming Period.

May I draw your attention to hollow at E as drawn.   The design
shows it as a lid on a pot so F must be smaller than E.   The shoulder
D gives it character and is important.   The whole job takes two or
three minutes to turn from the square, and if you take longer you
are slower than I am.   Elm is an easy wood to turn.   I've been

several times at exhibitions doing them, but it takes much longer to explain than to turn. Fig. 14 shows how much sideways the tool moves. When you try it make sure that you move the handle of the tool about, up and down as well as sideways. Don't use a very thin gouge or it will snap, or, if you do, at least avoid heavy cuts. Above all, don't say you cannot do it, for I've taught a blind man and he sells these lamps. His secret is that he feels the tools working; mine is that I prayed to be shown how to help him.

Here is a true story. The blind man wrote a letter to the Editor of the *Woodworker* and I was asked to answer it. It so happened that I was at a London store, and in my prayers I wished that I could show him. He turned up next day at the store from the wilds of Yorkshire. He only goes to London once a year, and he certainly did not know that I was going to be in London!

Alternative method. You can think in another way if you find this clock system of angles tedious, namely the middle of gouge rubbing the work, but the side of the gouge cutting. This means twisting the gouge as you follow round a curve so that the corners of the gouge are away from the work. Thus, in rounding a cylinder the gouge is lying level on the rest, but in turning a disc it is on its side. These remarks refer to gouges sharpened as Fig. 8 on page 57, and not to Fig. 7 which is all right so long as corner does not dig in. This twisting action must not be confused with sideways and up-and-down movements of the handle. Fig. 15, page 26, shows the tool at the correct twist and with the handle sideways.

Sometimes a long gentle curve done with a chisel results in the grain being torn out, just as planing against the grain is liable to tear the grain. Now a gouge will cut through the fibres rather than lift them up as a chisel does, but it must be moved along evenly. The more beautiful the wood the more curly it usually is. Furthermore the gentle curve shows up faults in the shape and in the finish of surface.

The movement of the gouge governs the shape but a $\frac{5}{8}$-in. shallow (G, Fig. 1) nicely fits the hollow of the toe of cabriole legs and also the toe and hollows in a twist leg before it is twisted. It does not lift the work as the hollows are near the centres of the lathe.

Cabriole leg. The best cabriole legs are shaped by hand, but you can make an inexpensive type entirely on the lathe. I deal with it more fully on page 101, but I give it here briefly as it exemplifies the use of the gouge. First we turn it as in Fig. 16, the wood running true between centres and the square left at one end. Now the foot end is put out of centre towards one corner of the leg for a square stool or table, and to one side if for a round stool or coffee table. The extent to which it is moved out of centre is half-way between true centre and the outside. The top end is put out of centre the other way so that the leg runs true where the round meets the square. Fig. 17 shows the idea.

The $\frac{5}{8}$-in. shallow gouge would be useful to do the toe with as it

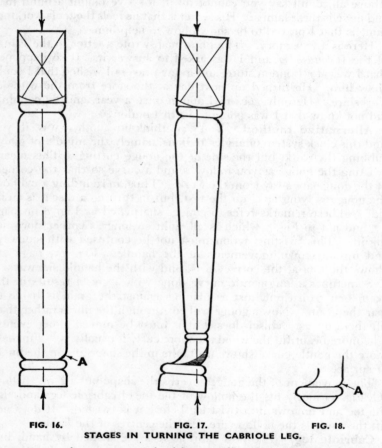

FIG. 16.   FIG. 17.   FIG. 18.

STAGES IN TURNING THE CABRIOLE LEG.

is not a continuous cut and with a smaller gouge you might get an uneven curve. The gouge is presented at 10.30 with the handle to the left and as you lift the handle twist it to 12. You may feel nervous that you may spoil it as it is not a continuous cut so hold the tool a bit more tightly and see that bevel is rubbing as you do it. Quite probably it will rub too much and you will see ribs where the tool starts each cut and wood has pushed it over. You ought also to feel it knocking.

The bead is not essential; in fact it weakens the leg. It only remains to re-chuck the leg to make it run true again and finish the toe as in Fig. 18. This makes it slide nicely on the carpet and also makes the toe not so liable to break off. The curve shown by the arrow can be much longer. It varies the look of the finished toe, and I suggest you vary it to see just how you like it.

Letting the bevel rub. Often I'm asked whether it is safe to use a gouge so high up on the work (Fig. 15) instead of holding it level to avoid digging in. It is absolutely a safe way of working

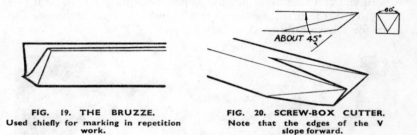

FIG. 19. THE BRUZZE.
Used chiefly for marking in repetition
work.

FIG. 20. SCREW-BOX CUTTER.
Note that the edges of the V
slope forward.

providing you let the bevel rub the work, but if the bevel is dubbed when sharpening and the tool has to have the handle lifted to enable it to cut then you will have trouble.

It would be as well for an instructor to show this principle with the work still and peep between bevel and work. If you start with the heel only on the work then lift handle to make it cut all is well. Care should be always taken, too, that the tool is on the rest before it touches the revolving work. In eagerness to work well on top of the work it may quite easily not touch. It is interesting to try it out though the tool may break or go through the window.

Bruzze. A buzz or bruzze is a tool that you need not buy. It is a V tool for marking the work where details come. We use it in repetition work but they are made so weak and generally lop-sided too that they are not much use. If you have one here are a few hints. When you sharpen it a little point is formed as in Fig. 19 caused by the slight hollow at the bottom of the V groove. If it is used on a metal rest it will probably slip sideways rather than go straight forward, so move it one way as you turn with it. This action is caused by one side cutting better than the other or by collisions of the two shavings (this can break it too).

In repetition work we hold it level and push it where grooves are worn in wooden rest.   For turning a pin at the end we tilt it on its side and this cuts the joint cleanly and does the pin as well.   A traveller said that we in High Wycombe were his only customers to-day for them, but some sets of tools include one.

There is a cutter very similar, Fig. 20, which is used in boxes for cutting external threads and cuts very cleanly indeed.   It must be sharpened as shown or it will not work.   The action is that the wood is forced towards the centre as it is being cut rather than lifted up. Perhaps you can understand it better if you realize that the top of the groove in the thread is cut before the bottom.   If the bottom were first the top of the groove would break away or lift off in a large chip.

Well you can take Westminster Abbey clock back now, and if you got into trouble breaking the minute hand off yours at home, I'm sorry for I have only tried to help.

FIG. 21. TURNING MAIN BODY OF THE VASE.
As a matter of interest you may like to know that I reckon to finish one of these from the rough square in 2 minutes.

CHAPTER 3 : USING THE CHISEL

MANY people think that a wood-turning lathe must go at a terrific speed, yet I know a pole lathe turner who completes a Windsor chair leg in 1 minute 20 seconds, complete with beads and

FIG. I.   HOW LONG SLENDER WORK ⎸S SUPPORTED.
Note how the left-hand thumb rests on the chisel, the ⎸ngers being taken right round
beneath the wood.

hollows, his speed being five revolutions forwards and backwards per movement of his leg as he works the treadle. The art of wood-turning is in paring off long, wide shavings with a chisel, or rope-like ones with a gouge, not a lot of dusty ones. We certainly do use speed, but the aim of this chapter is to show the mastery of wood-turning chisels, and speed will not help us to learn that.

Sharpening the chisel. Let us first sharpen the chisel. I deal with this fully in Chapter 5, but we can't do any turning until it is

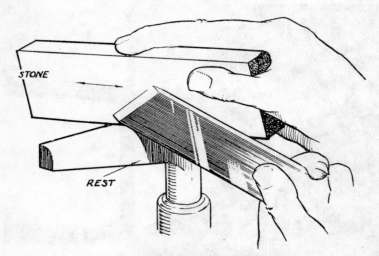

FIG. 2. SHARPENING CHISELS ON OILSTONE.
Note that the chisel is held on its side and remains stationary, the oilstone or oilstone slip being rubbed back and forth.

sharp. If it is new it will have a curved bevel (which is a mystery to me, as in the trade we use just a plain bevel on each side). There are two sorts you may buy; ordinary, and "long and strong" which is stouter in section. They range from $\frac{1}{8}$ in. to 4 in. wide. I suggest $\frac{1}{4}$-in. L and S, and $\frac{1}{2}$ in. either kind, $1\frac{1}{2}$-in. L and S, and a 2-in. ordinary. (If you want a 4 in. one, and can use it well, you can be excused from reading any more of this book.)

To grind the chisel an ordinary carborundum wheel mounted in the lathe is often used and is quite satisfactory, although a wet grindstone is preferred by many craftsmen. The thing to aim at is a nice even bevel, and if you can steady the handle against your body as you grind it is most helpful. My electric grinder is low and I steady the handle against my leg, taking care not to burn the steel.

I think the main trouble with carborundum wheels is that we use just what we come by (honestly I hope); yet before me is a book of 150 pages by the Carborundum people on grinding. If our wheel is too coarse it will be a job to get a good edge as, of course, it is what is left that cuts, not what we grind away. If the wheel glazes easily it is probably too hard, and the harder the steel the softer the stone to use. For carbide tools, which are extremely hard, the correct wheel is "Green Grit," which is quite friable and you can break pieces out of the wheel quite easily. I mention this about wheels as it is the reverse of what you might think. Still, carbide tools are not used for wood-turning. We use carbon steel which, when in the form of a file, is harder than high speed steel.

The oilstone. A lot of oil-stoning is not necessary, but please note that it is an *oil*-stone. If we do not use oil it will get clogged up and only burnish the tools (perhaps you go best well oiled?). Some like a little paraffin in the oil, and as long as we avoid thick, gummy oils all will be well. "Washita" stones were what we used, but like the "Arkansas" (which is an extremely good stone) they come from Oklahoma, U.S.A., and may be hard to come by. The manufactured ones we can get easily do not seem to give such a lasting edge, and my theory is this.

You will understand it better if you think how glass is cut by just a scratch with a diamond, yet the glass is fractured right through. I think there can be minute splits in the hard surface of steel, caused by too coarse a grinding wheel, or some sorts of oilstones. The idea is rather borne out by an oilstone in a rosewood case my father gave me. It was nothing more than Welsh slate, but it was the best stone I have ever had for getting a really fine edge. Now, Welsh slate is in layers. It is not a sandstone, so probably it did not score the steel so much as cut it. Slates vary in their capacity to cut, but mine was first rate.

When using an oilstone the oil should go black. My Dutch hone, which cost £5, soon makes the oil dark, which shows that it is cutting. The reason I mention it is that some of you may experiment with odd pieces of stone, and the speed with which the oil discolours is a sign of cutting. One of my men used a hard flooring tile from a church, and found it most excellent, and for four generations there was no Scottish blood in his veins to my knowledge. An 8 in. by 2 in. by 1 in. is the best size to use. The tool is held stationary, and *oilstone moved.* The tool rests against something, often on the tail-stock, and gradually the stone wears a flat on the tail-stock where it rubs. This practice is not to be recommended, but is how we do it, as it is just a handy height. Fig. 2 shows the operation. If the chisel is held on its edge as shown, it is easy to see whether the stone lies flat against the bevel.

The side of the oilstone is used for gouges, and it soon develops a hollow, an advantage in use. For chisels the wide, flat surface is used. This should be flat and true and when necessary it should be corrected by rubbing on a floor stone, or letting the sander in the factory true it up for you when the garnet paper is worn out. If you true a natural stone on a carborundum wheel it does not cut for some time, and a light is seen where it rubs as you do it. Still, I have often done it, and made a slip for a gouge out of a larger piece of oilstone.

We will put our oilstones carefully into a cigar box to keep the shavings, etc., from them, and give the chisels we have sharpened a

FIG. 3. USEFUL STROP FOR FINISHING OFF THE EDGE.
It is of leather glued to wood and dressed with oil.

rub on the piece of leather we have on a piece of wood as a strop. This strop is shown in Fig. 3. The rounded edges (they can vary) are handy for stropping the insides of gouges. If you did not have a box of cigars at Christmas, well I am sorry, but stones are best put somewhere away from dust; they can break or chip if dropped. If you wish to see whether your chisel is sharp, trail your thumb-nail along the edge and you will notice an even bite which is hard to describe, but I am sure you will get to know it if you wish to.

We do *not* oilstone tools to a shorter bevel than we grind them as is done with some plane irons and firmer chisels. I measured the angle on my own chisel and found it to be in the region of 43° as shown in Fig. 4. If your thumb-nail detects a gash (a sore place, I call it) along the edge you may be sure that it will mark the wood when in use. Another point is that if you turn wood which has been sandpapered this will put plenty of sore places on the tool edge, so do not sandpaper work until you have finished turning it.

Action of the chisel. First you should understand clearly how a chisel works. A chopper will help you better to grasp what I am trying to describe. You will notice when you chop up the firewood for the wife, that, after the edge has touched the wood, the sides of the chopper do the work; the cutting edge may not be doing anything

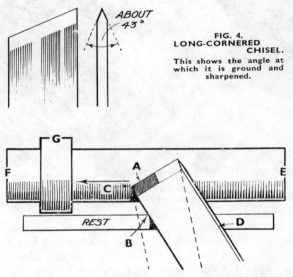

ABOUT
43°

FIG. 4.
LONG-CORNERED
CHISEL.
This shows the angle at which it is ground and sharpened.

FIG. 5. POSITION OF CHISEL FROM ABOVE WHEN TURN-ING CYLINDRICAL SHAPE.

at all. Now if you could force the chopper down at an angle to the line of cut, the chip would be bent or broken away, and the cutting edge would be rubbing hard against the wood all the time (if we could force the chopper down at all). This very principle explains why some wood-turners lose the cutting edge of their tools and say that the steel is of no use, for in turning the tools can be held so that the edge does most of the work. One test of a turner is the straightness of the shavings that come off. In using a chisel they should be like flat pieces of ribbon.

Practical work.   We will start work now.   The wood has been turned round with a gouge, and we will just chisel along so that the shaving comes off in one long ribbon.   Fig. 5 shows better than

FIG. 6.   FINISHING CYLINDER WITH THE CHISEL.
When the long-cornered chisel is used only the half near the heel is used.   See also Fig. 5.

words just how the tool is held.   At my works we once had a shaving fifty feet long.   You may not learn it as quickly as a boy I once saw at an Exhibition.   When I asked him if he would like a lesson in turning he replied, "No, thank you, teacher taught me all about

FIG. 7   HOW DIFFERENT PARTS OF REST COME INTO USE IN ACCORDANCE WITH TOOL BEING USED.

turning last week."   Still I am anxious that you should enjoy the sense of achievement that comes when you master the action of wood-turning tools.

It is not important where your hands are; if some other way suits

you well, do it that way.   It is how the tool is placed that matters
as that is what does the work; you only guide it.   As I am ambidextrous I reverse hands, and hold the tools either side of my body (my
body is large and it saves moving it), but many do not and get on

FIG. 8. ROUNDING OVER END OF CYLINDER WITH CHISEL.
Again only the heel portion is used.   Note that in both this and the operation in Fig. 6 the
bevel must rub on the wood.

just as well.   Fig. 5 shows a chisel which has been ground square
and one (dotted lines) ground "long cornered."   If you have two I
suggest a 2-in. wide chisel ground square across, and a 1½-in. one
ground long cornered.   If only one, the latter is the better as you
will see later on.

The cutting edge touches the wood at just the same angle as Fig. 5
shows.   You may have bought all of the chisel, but you must use
only part of it for this job.   If you want to learn quickly, just try
using the part that is not shaded.   The chisel will stab the work,
and, if a part of your hand is between the right-hand side (in sketch)
of the chisel and the rest, you will get a nasty nip, because this side
of the chisel is lifted up from the rest.   The part of the tool which
should do the work is the cutting edge at (A) or any part shown
shaded.   If too near (C), however, a feather of a shaving may form

at the left-hand corner to the side of the tool, and prevent the chisel from sliding along in the direction of the arrow. Sometimes it saves a ripple or a lot of twisted ribs on the work if we let (C) just cause a little feather of a shaving. This applies only to slender work.

The bevel of the tool is touching work that has been turned round previously. This is why you cannot start work at (E). Try it, and learn what happens. To turn (E) you face the tool the other way. The wood itself forms a sort of rest for the tool and the latter only touches the rest at (B). If your rest is uneven, this will prevent the tool from sliding nicely along, and the only thing is to put it right.

Now in the trade we prefer and use wooden rests for long jobs. Metal T rests are used for face turning or short work of large diameter. The rest becomes marked by small gouges, or by the chisel in doing various shapes, etc. If we do a lot of one pattern, quite pronounced grooves form in the wooden rest. These, however, do not in practice hinder the chisel from sliding along smoothly as Fig. 7 will explain. The part of the rest marked (G) is used for the chisel as we have to point the chisel more to the top of the work than we do with other tools which use the part marked (H). These notches that form are a help as they prevent tools skidding about, and is why we prefer wood for rests for turning, say, chair legs.

In Fig. 5 is a projecting detail marked (G). It may be only a bead, but we obviously cannot get the chisel edge at (A) cutting without the corner (C) bumping into this detail. We only have to ease the tool forward gradually so that (C) only is cutting. There may be a snag, however. The splitting action of the chisel may remove some of the bead in front of the cutting edge. If the wood is of that nature the thing to do is to cut the fibres with the point of a long-cornered chisel before turning the cylindrical part.

Long work between centres. Fig. 1 shows how I use my hands to steady long cylindrical work (not that a sample of long work is shown in the lathe). The chisel is moving to my right, towards the tail-stock, and my hand is around the work with the thumb on top of the chisel. Fig. 9 shows the idea more clearly. The handle of the tool is touching my side, and I can twist it so that it cuts. If it were flat on the rest it would not cut at all; if lifted too much it would cut a taper; or it might—Oh, darn well try yourself and find out what happens! As the bevel does not rub the work anything might occur, and that is just how you will learn. Your mistakes will teach you much more than success. The whole idea of putting your hand around the work is to steady it—it seldom wears through to the bone. In fact it is quite harmless and is a good thing to learn to do.

Another way of holding the chisel is with the thumb beneath

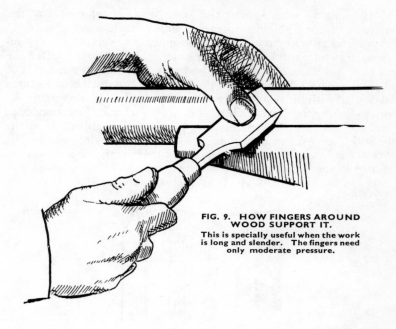

FIG. 9. HOW FINGERS AROUND WOOD SUPPORT IT.

This is specially useful when the work is long and slender.   The fingers need only moderate pressure.

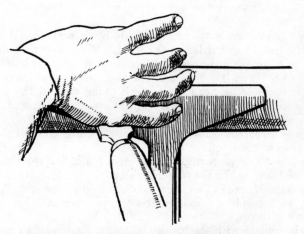

FIG. 10. FINGERS USED TO DEFLECT CHIPS.
This is useful if you find that you are put off by chips flying into your face.

and the fingers curled over the top.   Fig. 10 shows how the fingers can form a shield to prevent chips from flying.

Avoiding ribs in turning.   These appear as a sort of rough spiral on long or slender work, and can be caused in several ways.   Often the only cure is the use of a steady.   Some driving centres need a lot of tail-stock push to make them work, and some tail-stock centres burn and clog up with the result that the work tries to bend.   So forcing the work well on to the driving centre then easing it back a little may help.   First, however, put the centres into good condition and add oil to the tail-stock.   Perhaps your shaving is too wide, and moving your handle more to the left in Fig. 1 may help.   Also try having just a whisker of shaving at the leading corner of the tool.   You have, of course, sharpened the chisel with an even bevel, and allowed this to rub the work along the job.

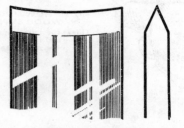

FIG. 11.   BODGER'S CHISEL.
Ground to a hollow shape to give a longer
cutting edge.

The tool can be made to act as a steady by being forced down, and making the bevel rub harder on the work.   This may well make the work try to come up and over the chisel, so just put your hand around the work to prevent it.   You are not likely to hold it there until it burns, whereas a steady can leave a burnt ring around the work.   A wedge of soft wood between the rest and the work may provide enough steadying action for the job, and will prevent the work from moving about in any direction.   Possibly the lathe is going too fast to allow a nice shaving to come off.

A man who has been turning longer than I, and had the Freedom of the City of London for his turning, talked with me about some golf club handles.   Neither of us knew how to avoid a little ribbing we saw in some, so a combined experience of 130 years did not solve it.   Still, don't give up.

My 2-in. chisel with its handle is 20 in. long, and to turn as in Fig. 5 I find my right hand is on the end of the handle at my side, and my left hand over the top of the chisel with the meaty part of the hand (which is on the other side of my hand to where I notice my thumb is) bearing against the rest. The fingers are curled round the chisel, and so can twist it to the right angle for turning. We always turn from larger to smaller diameter. If the chisel is lifted at (D), it takes more off the work, and that is how we govern those long curves in say a floor standard. Do not let your finger get between the chisel at (D) and the rest, unless you want to have a nip, for you certainly will if by chance you let the shaving come from the right-hand side of the chisel.

In Fig. 8 the chisel is being used to round over the end of a cylinder. Exactly the same movement is followed, the bevel of the tool rubbing the work all the time.

To chisel towards the right I suggest you move your body to the left, and use your hands just the same. It seems less natural, but to change hands may cause you never to quite master the movement.

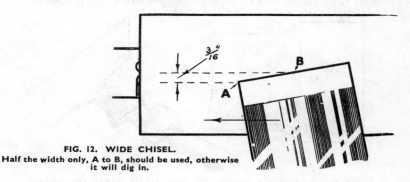

FIG. 12. WIDE CHISEL.
Half the width only, A to B, should be used, otherwise it will dig in.

You have to be so careful in describing turning. I once said to a man, "Change the tool round", and he caught hold of the chisel blade and held the handle on the rest asking what he should do next!

The bodger's chisel. The bodgers of Buckinghamshire who turn chair parts in the beech woods use a pole lathe, and one I know uses a chisel 2 in. wide as shown in Fig. 11. He grinds it to a hollow curve as this gives it a longer cutting edge on curved work such as the bulbous part of a leg or on the underframing of chairs. The shavings he removes are $1\frac{1}{2}$ in. or so wide, and, when you consider that his power is only his own foot pulling down on a piece of string tied to the branch of a tree above, it is not bad going.

Now I don't advise you to grind your chisel so, except as an experiment, as it causes it to dig in more easily, but if you are going to use a Bodger's lathe (which is another name for a pole lathe)

4—P.W.T.

you will find it an advantage because of its slow speed of five revolutions for one push of the treadle. He has told me it is lovely in the woods at 4 a.m., but I should have thought the second line of "It's nice to get up in the morning" would have applied.

Wide chisels.   Now I like wide chisels, 2 in. or more across, but they are expensive and not to be found in many tool shops. So let us have a few thoughts on wide chisels (thinking is not harmful, although some seem to manage without it). As I'm often at Exhibitions I bring mine out. It is 2 in. wide and 20 in. long, including its split handle, and I swank by taking off shavings, and have been photographed with shavings right across the stand. If any of my workmen were around, however, I would not do it as it is so simple to use. One man at the works brought off a shaving 50 ft. long.

I will try to show you why a 2-in. chisel is useful to have, and why, although it is all yours, you must use only half of its width, (A) to (B) in Fig. 12. Please don't take my word for it, but try it and see what

FIG. 13. (A) CURVED SHOULDER CUT WITH STRAIGHT CHISEL. (B) SHOWING HOW STRAIGHT-EDGE LIES FLAT ON TWIST BIT.

happens. You can, of course, turn it over and use the other part of chisel to the right, but the sketch shows the tool moving to the left.

So we have an inch of cutting edge at an angle, and the shaving can come off anywhere in that inch. This position is maintained by keeping the tool at the same projection from the rest, letting the meaty part of the hand rub the rest as we slide the tool along.

You may understand the point I am trying to explain better if you realize that this 1 in. of cutting edge has only $\frac{3}{16}$ in. play forward or backward before you are in trouble. The dotted lines in Fig. 12 help to explain the point. You have to maintain this position of the tool against the cut, as of course the wood tends to force the tool towards you. You can increase the safe distance by twisting the tool to a greater angle, but it does not give so clean a cut.

Straight lines on curves.   It is an interesting point (although of no practical value) that the wood is of curved shape where being turned although the chisel is straight, as in Fig. 13 (A).   The greater the angle at which it is held the more the wood is curved.   A straight-edge will touch the entire curve of a Jennings bit if held across it at an angle as shown in Fig. 13 (B).   Thus we have the curious feature that a straight edge can form a curve.   However, all this is getting hypothetical rather than practical.

You will realize that a narrow chisel has to be kept more in the

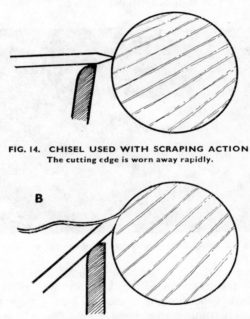

FIG. 14.   CHISEL USED WITH SCRAPING ACTION
The cutting edge is worn away rapidly.

FIG. 15.   CORRECT METHOD OF USING THE CHISEL.
Long shavings are removed resulting in a cleaner finish.
The cutting edge lasts much longer.

correct place than a wide one, and that is why the latter is easier to use; also, being heavier, it damps out vibration and is easier to hold too.   Everything is in its favour except the price, availability, and the fact that it needs room to work on, but it is worth having if you are serious.

Some books advise you to use a plane to turn with.   Well, the principle is all right, but I see no advantage, and have never used one. Barbers use a cut-throat razor for their enjoyment, whereas we use safety razors and mowing machines, so let's be professional in turn-ing and use the naked blade of steel, and get a lovely clean cut.

You may have such a curly grained piece of wood that the chisel just splinters up the wood in the same way that a hand plane will. A gouge may solve your difficulty. This cuts through the fibres of the wood in a different way from a chisel, and you will better see this point if you cut a curve as in Fig. 13 (A) with the chisel and then cut one with the gouge. The chisel tends to lift the fibres whereas a gouge cuts through them. Try it for yourself. Words are not so good as actions to find out what happens.

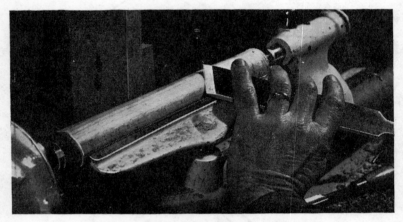

FIG. 16. ENLARGED VIEW OF HOW CHISEL IS HELD.

A gouge would scarcely be suitable to shave with as it would cause grooves in the face, and fibres stand up on mine anyhow. So our gouge will leave grooves, but these are better than pieces being splintered out on troublesome wood.

Letting the bevel rub. In all chisel work the bevel must rub the work just as I explained for the gouge. It prevents the tool from digging in. There is more in it than that, however. Fig. 14 shows the chisel used with a scraping action and it is clear that the wood acts as a sort of grindstone and takes off the edge quickly. When used in the proper way as in Fig. 15 the chisel cuts the wood and the shavings pare off sweetly on top. Used in this way the cutting edge will last a lot longer.

CHAPTER 4 : SCRAPING

AFTER having told you so often about cutting wood as it prefers to be cut, I now have to speak about wood as it does not mind being cut, to wit, scraping it. Let me say at once, however, that it is not good practice for spindle turning, that is, work between centres, although it is for face turning. One of my friends has several tons of ebony, boxwood, and rosewood, for he is an exotic wood merchant, and much of this will be turned by scraper tools, because it does not mind such treatment. To me it is a far less interesting way of turning. Ordinary spindle turning demands movement of tools in

FIG. I. INK POT IN IMITATION OF BELL.
This is a good example of work which must be scraped in parts.

three directions, whereas in this scraping action the tool moves rather in one plane only.

The great advantage is that fine detail work can be easily done without much skill, but only suitable wood should be treated in this way. One school for instructors advocates scraping cuts for safety reasons. Well, if my advice is followed there is no danger at all in learning

45

to turn properly.   I wonder whether girls are taught to cook in the refrigerator to save burning themselves?

Where scraping is essential.   Now, I turned a number of ink-pots from some old oak beams from a belfry and I had to scrape parts of them.   Fig. 1 shows the design, and you just cannot turn parts of it any other way.   First I turned it with a gouge to the general shape of the bell, then with a sharp-pointed tool cut each side of the little beads (see A, Fig. 1).   A file was ground just a little narrower than the space between the beads, and it was left just as it was from the grinding wheel with a slight burr on it.   This removed the wood and did not damage the beads.   As it was

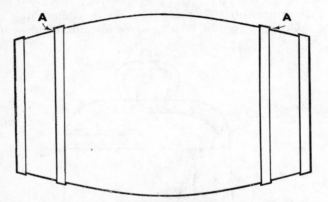

**FIG. 2.   SMALL BARREL WHICH NEEDS SCRAPING TO FINISH
CLEANLY.**
After the general shape has been turned with gouge and chisel the
corners of the bands need to be scraped, especially at (A).

narrower a slight sideways movement for the final cut removed any lines the rough edge might have left on the surface of the work.

The inside was hollowed out with a scraper tool because end grain wood works nicely this way.   It is much easier to cut a true hole if the tool rests flat on the rest.   The tool tries to bob up and down a bit, so you rest your elbow on the tail-stock, and all is well.   The lid was fitted and was turned as a solid job between centres.   Some had hand-carved tops or cannons such as old bells have.   Modern bells are bolted to a flat surface on the headstock, which is much more mechanical, but not so nice to look at.

Barrels are another job where a scraper tool is necessary, for a chisel to cut corner (A, Fig. 2) cleanly it must touch the wood.   Can a chisel cut at all if it does not touch the wood, you may well say!

Now, if you have followed previous chapters you will have seen that the leading corner and to about half way along the cutting edge only must be allowed to cut; also that we must always cut from larger diameter to smaller.   So to turn corner (A) we must either cut like sharpening a pencil the wrong way from the point end, or let the trailing corner do it, and then it will dig in nicely!   So here again a scraping tool helps us.   Some barrels are turned with grooves for bands, but this does not look so well.

If the wood is not of a fibrous nature you can turn it all right by first using the chisel to cut to one corner, then turning it over to cut to the other.   Great skill will be needed to make the line of barrel follow through nicely, and it would certainly look bad if it did not do so.   You will gain most help from these notes if you try out the ways wood prefers to be cut, and also see how the tool digs in.

I have advised my daughter, who is going to Africa, to watch and see whether the top or bottom jaw moves in an alligator and crocodile, for I think they work a different way, but she says, "I'll just run when I see one."   Perhaps it does not matter, but the way wood wants to be cut and how to prevent tools digging in, does matter to a wood turner.   Sometimes a piece of turning seems nice but has a little corner that wants removing, and you feel that you may spoil it by using the chisel again.   This is a real fear as it is difficult to take just a little off with the chisel, especially if it is none too sharp.   Well, we do just lay the chisel flat on the rest and scrape with it for safety's sake, but don't get into the bad habit of scraping the wood to shape when it can be properly turned.

Angle of scraping tool.   I was explaining to some choir-boy friends how unhygienic it is to kiss young ladies.   "Yes, I know, for Daphne smacked my face," said one, "but she kissed it better."   Well, scraper tools can do the same, and a blind man who came to me broke a heavy file in three pieces and cut himself just because he would not let it trail a little.   He was told several times how dangerous it was to point it upwards, but simply would do it his way.

The blind man whom I taught has turned six sackfuls of bowls, and writes that he does it nicely using the gouge for the insides.   His worry is that his polishing is not good enough, though he sells them.   I mention all this both as a warning and as an encouragement (I honestly believe kissing is all right—in fact, my wife of blessed memory sometimes made me late for work because of it).

Some are worried about the height of the rest in face-plate turning and spindle turning.   Well, it does not matter, but see that the tool slopes down a little when scraping.   Then when it cuts it goes away from the work, and it won't smack your face.   The idea is shown in Fig. 3. In spindle turning, of course, the bevel of the tool rests on the work, and that prevents it from digging in, which is a different principle.

Fine work. Now, such things as tiny knobs for miniature cabinets, pegs for violins, and so on are often done in boxwood, and here small scraping tools are ideal. It is advisable to oilstone these tools, as a burr is not wanted, but oilstone the bevel last. A hard marble-like stone is needed. Arkansas is ideal, but is an awful price. Still, for serious fine work I do think it worth acquiring one. Why not let a friend know when your birthday is?

The skill in turning these small items is in knowing how much pressure to apply, for a hollow in the neck of a knob would require

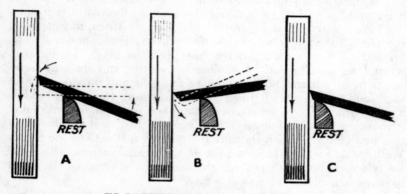

FIG. 3. POSITION OF SCRAPING TOOL.
(A) shows how tool is liable to dig in if caught in wood. At (B) the tool runs away from the wood if it catches in. Although the tool slopes up at (C) the rest is close to the work and there is no great leverage.

more than that needed in just rounding a bead. So here is another case of handling tools gently rather than using brute force.

Practice cuts. Now as you wait at the dinner-table just draw in ink on the tablecloth a few simple designs, then grip, say, a knife and pretend that the edge of the table is the rest. (With the choir-boy in mind, however, perhaps it would be better not to use ink for hygienic reasons.) Your left hand can hold the blade with the thumb underneath (which I find most natural), and with your right hand just move the handle about to follow the design. What I want you to discover is how you can push the blade forward, compressing the parts of your left hand against the table edge. You will find for larger curves it is better to grip between the fingers, but let part of the hand near the wrist-watch touch the table edge. It is a controlled movement that we are trying to get, and this action of one hand against the rest, while the other moves the tool about is ideal for this sort of face turning.

The pair of rosewood candlesticks (Fig. 4) were done in this way circa A.D. 1908, but carved by the boy next door. They are not given as an example of good design, but I'm proud of them as I was a youngster then. The central part is a copy of a silver cup you can win by sailing your yacht round the Isle of Wight. It is a good thing to keep your eyes open for nice combinations of curves, and it will surprise you in the way it will broaden your outlook on what to turn. When in business I always looked in antique shops, some of which had old stuff in them, and in those days people introduced such work into the job, whereas modern stuff is designed so that it can easily be sanded smooth in a machine.

Those who have to turn large diameter work will find scraping tools a help —I'm thinking of pattern makers in particular. Their trouble is that the shape must be true to a template, and it is often

FIG. 4. CANDLESTICK IN ROSEWOOD TURNED MANY YEARS AGO.

built up with wood which has the grain in various directions.

Scraping tools. Some people like to buy ready-made tools. I've a set myself made specially for brass finishers, as shown in Fig. 5. Files are quite all right, however, or, for very small work, pieces of band-saw blade. You certainly will find yourself using just two or three and find the movement of the hands provide all the curves you need. Should your aspirations rise to making a set of chessmen, I do suggest that you grind tools to suit the main curves, and just push them in. Then all will be alike.

For some woods such as elm you can use the scraper direct from the grinding wheel. Other woods need the tool to be finished off on the oilstone. In all cases the top serrations of the file are ground away first, and the edge ground to the required shape *afterwards*.

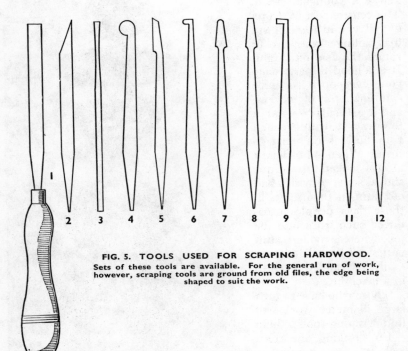

FIG. 5. TOOLS USED FOR SCRAPING HARDWOOD.

Sets of these tools are available. For the general run of work, however, scraping tools are ground from old files, the edge being shaped to suit the work.

Sometimes you get a better result using a scraping tool finished with a ticketer. This turns up the edge just as a cabinet maker's scraper is sharpened. The method of sharpening is described on page 61.

Incidentally the inside of a bowl is always finished with the scraper (see page 86). It is a help to grind several files to various shapes to suit the curvature of the bowl.

CHAPTER 5 : SHARPENING TURNING TOOLS

"IT is not what you grind away that counts, but what you leave", might be a good slogan for this chapter. Boys will quite happily make the sparks fly when grinding a knife and then blame the steel as being of no use because the blade bends and won't take an edge. A wiser boy might ask me to sharpen it, whereupon I would ask him what he wished to cut.

FIG. I. GRINDING A GOUGE ON A DRY GRINDING WHEEL.
Be careful to avoid burning the edge.

How tools cut. Now for a moment let us consider cutting edges. I know that we don't use knives, etc. in wood turning but it will help in understanding the problem if we think also of the other tools. A bread knife has a notched edge and cuts bread well, but if used on cheese it would certainly not cut cleanly at all. In the first case we have a sawing action whereas the cheese needs more of a cutting action. We don't use a saw when doing wood turning, I can hear you say, but consider, what is the difference? It is chiefly that in turning it is that the wood is moving, not the tool. The action is partly cutting as we cut cheese and partly sliding along as in cutting bread.

Let us now sharpen my lady's scissors. We file or grind them, not oilstone them. The reason is that we want the fibres of cotton to catch in the slight roughness caused by the grinding wheel or file and not slide away and avoid being cut.

If the above has set you thinking it will do no harm but the problem is not quite so simple as it first seems. The turning tools you buy *will not be ground as they should be*. The gouge will have too long a bevel and the chisels a curved bevel. Don't ask me why. It is one of those curious conventions. Every new turning chisel I have seen has had a curved bevel; yet no practical turner ever uses it so. A flat bevel is always used. I mention this because you might well think that you could not go wrong if you retained the rounded bevel.

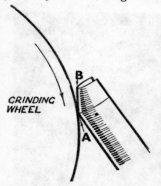

GRINDING
WHEEL

FIG. 2   GRINDING GOUGE.
The heel bears against the wheel first.

Grinding. Fig. 1 shows how I grind a gouge. I am standing quite firmly with the wheel at a height that suits me. My right hand is against my side and can rotate the gouge while my other hand steadies itself on the rest and forms a place for gouge to rest in. I should grip a chisel and slide it across the surface of the wheel, but neither hand moves about much. Thus a nice even bevel results. Some might prefer to have the rest at an angle but I find that this way suits me best.

I start to grind as in Fig. 2. The cutting edge is away from the wheel and is not spoilt. I then raise the handle until I feel the bevel nicely resting on the wheel. You can also see the sparks coming down the top surface of the tool whereas before they mostly passed beneath. Little pressure is used and no harm is done such as burning the edge, although some old craftsmen might prefer a sandstone wheel which is just an ordinary grindstone running in water. When using this pressure *is* needed. It seems to me so wet and mucky, however, that only boys and comedians would appreciate it.

I can hear the old craftsman saying "the edge will stay longer if ground on a grindstone" and this is true. Consider a diamond glass cutter. A split will go right through the glass but only a scratch shows on the surface. Well, it may be that your fast-cutting corundum wheel has caused a lot of scratches in your tool and that these are deeper than is apparent from the appearance. Still your humble servant avoids grinding to the extreme cutting edge which is oilstoned only, not ground.

Grinding wheels are certainly made in a large variety for special jobs, coarse and fine; also hard and soft bonding. My bandsawyer once sawed a stone in half, yet it was the proper wheel for sharpening some wide machine plane irons. Some are for use with a cooling liquid or they will burn the steel, so don't use any old wheel and then condemn grinding wheels as useless for the purpose.

Oilstones. Let us think about oilstones now. My father gave me a stone in a rosewood case, and it was a wonderful stone for giving a fine edge. On asking what it was, he told me "Welsh slate". Now if he had called it a fine argillaceous rock of the Cambrian period containing small colourless mica in size 6,000 to the inch I should have been more impressed. Its layer formation might have explained why it cuts rather than scores the surface. When I was in North Wales I saw mountains made of it, and they are probably there now, but it varies immensely, and I do think someone ought to make tests in different places to find a sort that does sharpen tools. Marble too is often worth experiment.

A barber once sold me a Dutch hone. It shows a black smear in the oil when used indicating that steel is being removed, yet it is so smooth that it could scarcely scratch. It is similar to Arkansas stone which comes from U.S.A. Another good stone is the Washita which is a bit coarser and most suitable for our use. It is difficult to buy washita stones to-day in Britain. All this is perhaps rather ideal; most of you will use a manufactured stone. If you do, use the fine grade.

Oilstoning a chisel. More important than the kind of stone is how you use it. The way I describe is for *wood turners* not carpenters or cabinet makers. The aim is not to shorten the bevel nor dub it over because in turning it has to rub the work. If we make a little short oilstone bevel such as that in an ordinary woodworking chisel we must lift the handle end of the tool to make it cut, but as only a short bevel is rubbing the work it digs in. You can use force and make it stay where you want it to, but it is so much nicer to turn properly and let the tools just do it themselves.

Once when I was swanking at an exhibition (confession is good for the soul) I said "you only have to move the tools about and they do the work themselves." "Yes, for you, but not for us", said a man, and a chorus of six said "So say all of us". Well it seems each one had sharpened his tools with the oilstone on the bench, moving the tool along it, and I believe that was the trouble. In the trade we generally run the oilstone along the top of the tail-stock, the tool resting against the tightening bolt that stands up as in Fig. 3. Of course it spoils the look of it so why not fix up a post or find a place that suits the job?

We want a place to slide the oilstone (preferably 8 in. × 2 in. ×

FIG. 3. SHARPENING CHISEL WITH OILSTONE.
The chisel is supported on its side and is held stationary. The oilstone is held flat against the bevel and rubbed back and forth.

1 in.) which is at a natural height to suit us, and a place to rest the chisel against. We slide the oilstone backwards and forwards in a straight line with just a little oil on it, but rubbing it on the back part of the bevel away from the cutting edge. Then as we get going nicely we can move the chisel so that the oilstone rests nicely flat on the bevel, and the little oil shows clearly what we are doing. Too much oil would be inclined to hide the tool. Later we can feel how the oilstone is and then we need not look so much.

The chief trouble in sharpening turning tools is to remove the burr caused by the grinding wheel, and that is why I don't grind quite to the edge if I can help it.   A coarse oilstone also puts a burr on (sometimes we can use this to advantage).

Testing.   Let us now see how to test the edge with the fingers. As you progress you will know when tools need sharpening.   At the works where we would turn 2 gross of chair legs a day, probably four or five tools would be used and they would be ground once a

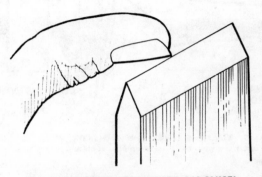

FIG. 4.   DETECTING KEEN EDGE ON CHISEL.
The finger- or thumb-nail is drawn along the edge.

day.   Some work of course might call for more frequent grinding, whereas for some beech jobs they might last for days.   In a large shop where they had fourteen lathes it was quite usual for one grind on a wet sandstone or grindstone to last the day, and this on bone dry wood.

I mention this because a lot of unnecessary grinding takes place because people *won't cut wood as it prefers to be cut.*   If you merely scrape the edge is lost in no time.   I mentioned earlier about a saw action in cutting.   Well, oak can make an edge sore or rough, and if we turned beech afterwards it would show scratches on the work. But this sore edge or one with a bite in it is ideal for cutting cleanly through the fibres of oak.   Fig. 4 shows how to detect this bite. So I don't advocate too much oilstoning and as long as no burr exists all is well.   In fact we sometimes don't oilstone at all for turning oak.   When beech and oak jobs are to be turned the beech one is done first.   So for beech, and of course similar woods a nice smooth edge is wanted and the finger-nail can detect it.   It is surprising how a small notch, quite undetected by eyesight, can cause a mark on beech.

A chisel used to turn a slight hollow as in Fig. 5 needs the corner of the bevel removed or it will score the work. Only the corner is removed. It is not ground away up to the point. It is used only for a slight hollow as a chisel does these much more cleanly than a gouge would.

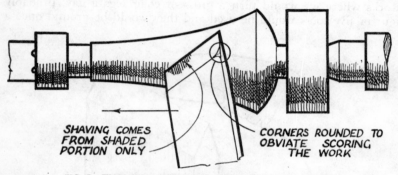

SHAVING COMES FROM SHADED PORTION ONLY

CORNERS ROUNDED TO OBVIATE SCORING THE WORK

FIG. 5. TURNING SHALLOW HOLLOW WITH CHISEL.
Unless the corner is removed it bears on the wood and scores an unsightly mark.

Grinding a gouge. Gouges are certainly ground in all sorts of ways. One of my men ground his obliquely (see Fig. 6) so that he was opposite the work with the tool held slightly sideways. So if you see some tools ground not as stated here, well don't worry; it takes all sorts to make a world. Let us consider our $\frac{3}{4}$-in. or 1-in. roughing-out gouge. It is ground square across as in Fig. 7, and it

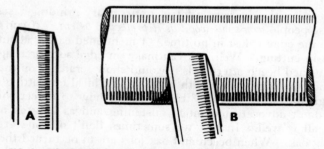

FIG. 6. GOUGE GROUND AT ANGLE FOR ROUGHING OUT

needs its corners left projecting as much as the rest of the edge. Fig. 1 shows exactly how I would grind it, just twisting the handle and resting the end as shown, giving a nice even true bevel. If you have a small L and S gouge, say $\frac{3}{8}$ in. for face plate or bowl work that too is ground square across (see Chapter 8 for why).

But spindle work demands a different end to the gouge (except in the roughing-out gouge) and a lot depends on whether we wish to do hollows nearly the size of gouge or larger hollows. Briefly, if the gouge seems too large for the hollow make it more pointed. This makes a smaller length of cutting edge but is not so troublesome to use. Fig. 8 shows clearly just how to grind them, but be sure when grinding that you are looking at the actual cutting edge, not a burr of steel which when oilstoned away leaves the tool quite another shape. Men in the trade like a lathe with a wood bed, and the usual thing is to jab the tool into it to push this false edge or burr away.

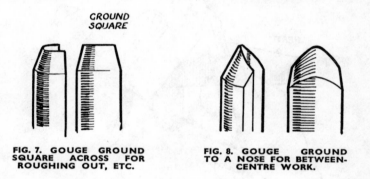

GROUND
SQUARE

FIG. 7. GOUGE GROUND
SQUARE ACROSS FOR
ROUGHING OUT, ETC.

FIG. 8. GOUGE GROUND
TO A NOSE FOR BETWEEN-
CENTRE WORK.

You cannot do this with a metal lathe bed, but you can push the tool into any block of wood.

With continuous use a series of hollows is worn into the edge of the oilstone and these are helpful. Be careful not to round over the bevel. The inside is not so important and the only difficulty is to remove the burr cleanly. The gouge is rested on the tail-stock or post, and the oilstone rubbed up and down with a bit more pressure on the cutting edge as in Fig. 9. You can if you like just hold the gouge in the hand and move the oilstone up and down. Gouges are not so fussy as chisels, but the bevel rubs on the work just the same.

The buzz or bruzze needs both sides balanced in grinding and this is quite a test in grinding. The tool is not essential, however. There should be a little point at the bottom of the V because of the small hollow in the tool. This seems to help the tool in working. Fig. 10 shows better than words just what to look for. These tools always seem too light in section and break off occasionally which must be good for the tool trade (or is it?). They make them lop-sided

5—P.W.T.

too, and I don't think anyone is keen on them, but for repetition work in the furniture trade they have their uses (or used to have before automatics began to do repetition work).

Scraping tools. We will now consider scraping tools made out of files, and let me say at once we use them as they are without altering the temper, for all thick files are softer inside and are ideal.

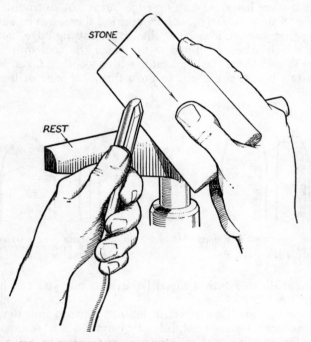

FIG. 9. SHARPENING THE GOUGE AGAINST THE REST.
The gouge is held stationary against the rest and the stone moved across it. The gouge is gradually revolved so that all parts of the edge are sharpened. The bevel is kept flat.

They are not liable to snap off if you use thick ones. The bevel is not important but it is certainly not acute—in fact it could be nearly square across. The side view, E, Fig. 12 shows it. This would absorb heat from the cutting edge and also give it better support. There is no need for a long bevel in any case. The bevel does not rub the work as the paring cut of a chisel would do. I find the shape (C) is nice for bowl turning, etc., but the scrapers can be ground to suit the job in hand. A set of tools used for brass turning is shown on page 50, and might please those who want to do small scraper work in the lathe in such nice woods as box or ebony. These tools are used just as we buy them, and I suggest that the only burr needed is that caused by the oilstone, so oilstone the bevel *after* rubbing the face.

By trailing your thumb across the surface of the tool as in Fig. 11 you can feel this little burr catching your skin, but for bowl turning in elm or oak we need a larger and coarser burr such as that caused by the grinding wheel.

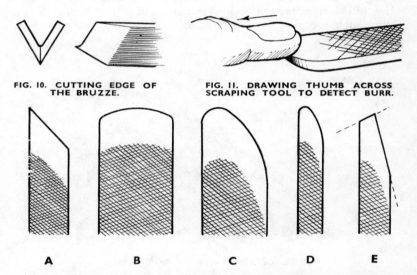

FIG. 10. CUTTING EDGE OF THE BRUZZE.

FIG. 11. DRAWING THUMB ACROSS SCRAPING TOOL TO DETECT BURR.

A   B   C   D   E

FIG. 12. SCRAPING TOOLS GROUND TO VARYING SHAPES FROM OLD FILES
The shape is made to suit the work in hand. Note how the top is ground off at a slight angle.

Grinding. I hold the file which I'm grinding in much the same way as in Fig. 1, but at a much less bevel, and for sides of curves I push it up higher on the wheel as Fig. 13 shows. The same result could be got by moving the end in a circle or arc, but it is more involved in the movement required than laying the tool over a little and pushing it up on the wheel.

Just a word of warning on grinding anything held freely in the hand as I am doing in Fig. 1. To grind an ordinary chisel or gouge with a bevel is all right but grinding a tool nearly square across could cause a dig into the wheel and give trouble. In any case it would chatter and kick if pressed too heavily. So perhaps you would prefer to have the tool supported on the rest or the little flat platform provided on grinding machines.

The burr is caused by the wheel and is probably the result of the sparks burning themselves back on to the edge.   So we grind the bevel last and that is all there is to it.   You can grind it for too long a period, however, so that instead of a neat burr you have quite a mess on the top of the tool and this won't cut.   Just once round on the wheel seems right for the final grind.   Stroke your finger off the edge to detect it, and learn just what is best for the job in hand.

Use of the ticketer.   Beech, sycamore, and similar woods do not require such a coarse burr as elm, oak, and some mahogany, etc.

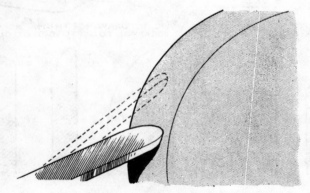

FIG. 13. GRINDING FILE ON THE WHEEL.

and here we want a "ticketed" edge such as cabinet-makers have on their scrapers.   We first oilstone the edge with the finest stone so that there is no burr and we test it with the fingers.   A "bite" when you run the finger-nail along the edge is desirable.   Now with a ticketer, which may be any $\frac{1}{4}$-in. dead hard steel rod, we bend the edge over.   First we rub the ticketer on top of the tool with heavy pressure, then on the bevel with pressure rather on edge, as in Fig. 14. You should have a smooth edge, but some steel won't ticket and some ticketers are not hard or smooth enough.

I once carried out a test on forty-eight steels for a steel-maker to find the best to use for a tool to be ticketed.   The best was from Swedish iron turned into steel and used very soft indeed.   The action of ticketing it seemed to harden the edge, and it bent up easily.   It is a subject needing research.   A German maker and

French maker of hand scrapers may come to the mind of an older craftsman.

It's a mystery what makes good scraper steel. In many ways steel is a mystery in any case. In my tool box is a thick file sawed through with a soft steel bandsaw with no teeth on it, like sawing a file in two using the back of a hand saw. Friction saws run very fast indeed and pressure is needed, but it is the hard file that suffers not the soft saw blade! Now cast steel or carbon steel as used in

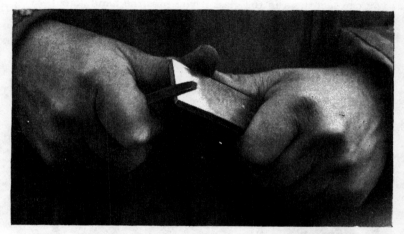

FIG. 14. TURNING EDGE OF SCRAPING TOOL WITH TICKETER.
A hard steel rod is used to turn the edge similarly to that of a cabinet-maker's scraper.

razors is harder than high speed steel, but engineers don't use cast steel tools so much because high speed steel is so much better for retaining its edge. There are qualities in steel besides hardness, and one maker of cold chisels claims that it can be forced through two and a half inches of mild steel, and when blunt can be filed sharp again.

This is mentioned because I've been told we are behind the times and we ought to use tipped tools which have an extremely hard insert of carbide in them. These tools quite happily turn the hard scale of cast iron off at good speed, but their cutting edge is weak if made thin and easily breaks, and that would be like turning with tools made of glass which would be hard but brittle.

In plain English if your tools won't keep sharp they are probably all right, but you are holding them at work wrongly or running the lathe far too fast *without removing any wood*, and just wearing them away. To temper them harder would not help much—in fact the edge might break away. Often a heavier cut enables a tool to keep sharp longer, for the pressure and hard rubbing is further back than the extreme cutting edge, but don't try it when shaving.

Just a final word; the sparks from a grinding wheel can burn themselves into glasses so stand sideways to avoid them if they are liable to come near. Of course they are harmful to the eyeballs too. A piece of glass held in the stream of sparks will show clearly afterwards as you can feel them in the glass if you pass the hand across.

LARGE PATTERN BEING TURNED ON A SMALL LATHE.
The machine is the Coronet Major, and a special pulley has been incorporated to reduce the r.p.m. to a rate suitable for the work.
By courtesy of the Coronet Tool Co.

CHAPTER 6 : PRONG CHUCKS, CENTRES, STEADIES

A FURNITURE manufacturer once told me he always kept "Ginger" wild because he did more work that way. Well, centres in a wood-turning lathe that will not drive, or are always burning, can make one wild, and throwing the wood across the shop does not help very much. So let us have a few thoughts on what is required of these centres, for, of the large number of lathes I have come across in fifty years of turning, only one lathe manufacturer sends out the centres as we use them in High Wycombe.

Prong chuck. It is obvious that the purpose of the prong chuck is to rotate the wood. It seems unnecessary to mention it, but so many gradually wear and develop faults that prevent them from doing their work. When a prong chuck fails to be satisfactory the usual plan is to sharpen its fangs. This makes its central point relatively

FIG. I. THREE VIEWS OF PRONG CHUCK, SHOWING HOW IT CAN BE TRUED WITH A FILE GROUND TO A SPECIAL SHAPE.

longer, and if too long or fat it will prevent the chuck from penetrating the wood, because the fangs cannot reach without undue strain being put on the lathe by screwing up the tail-stock centre extra hard. This centre then starts to make the wood burn and we blame it, whereas the blame should be on the other end.

When a centre is always burning look first to the chuck end to see what is wrong. There are three main faults we may find: the point is too long or fat; the space between the point and fangs needs filing away; or the fangs are too blunt. The first fault can be cured by putting the T rest near to it, and turning it with the end of a file suitably ground for the job as in Fig. 1. It is advisable to run the lathe not too fast. The cutting edge of the file is as shown, not as when we turn wood. The tool is moved forward at centre height as in the sketch which is a side view of the job. The shape of the tool is a small radius to suit the hollow which is between the point and fangs.

This brings us to the second fault, that of the space between point and fangs needing to be filed away (if we cannot manage to turn it away when we are touching up the point). Some chucks have no space and so long as nothing prevents the point and fangs from penetrating wood it is all right. Most people give the fangs far too sharp a bevel, or even put a bevel both sides. Some makes of chuck are such poor stuff they bend backwards in use; and some turners

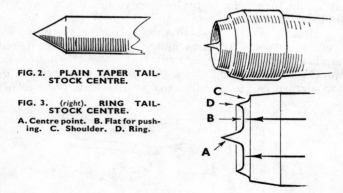

FIG. 2.   PLAIN   TAPER   TAIL-
         STOCK CENTRE.

FIG. 3.   (right).   RING   TAIL-
         STOCK CENTRE.
A. Centre point. B. Flat for push-
    ing. C. Shoulder. D. Ring.

catch their tools on them in use. Aim at making the driving face flat, and the trailing angle at about 45°.

In the trade the lathe is seldom stopped. Instead the tail-stock centre is eased back and the hand put around the wood which should stop. This is a good policy as small A/C motors do not like a lot of stopping and starting. If the wood hangs on the chuck end and perhaps flies out when tail-stock centre is eased back look for a burred or bent fang. The remedy is obvious. So if your lathe will not easily give up driving the work when you slacken the back centre do not get nervous. Try to find out why. If you keep your hand round the work no harm will come to you.

Tail-stock centre. Let us now consider the tail-stock centre. We use two types; a plain taper of 60° such as engineers use, best for heavy work such as 10-in. squares in hard oak (Fig. 2), and the ring centre (Fig. 3). The home craftsman will find the latter the more suitable. It is here where some manufacturers slip up, for they do not realize that the job of this centre is to *push*. They remove the very part of centre that could push. A taper point in use works its way into the end grain; so will a ring, and we have to give the tail-stock wheel another turn. Often we give it too much, so straining the lathe and causing the centre to start burning. Fig. 3 shows a good ring centre. The flat part between point and ring can push the wood against the prong chuck and will not penetrate nor burn.

Fig. 3 is enlarged to show the idea more clearly. A diameter of $\frac{1}{4}$ in. to $\frac{5}{8}$ in. would be the two limits probably for general use. Now (A) is the point and does not project too much from the ring. It would depend on the wood to be turned generally speaking. The softer the wood the longer it should be for centering purposes. The part (B) pushes and when it has pushed and still more pressure is

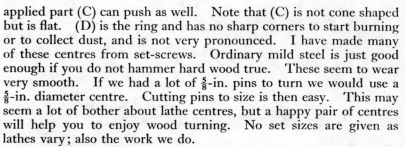

FIG. 4. FOUR-PRONGED CHUCK.

applied part (C) can push as well. Note that (C) is not cone shaped but is flat. (D) is the ring and has no sharp corners to start burning or to collect dust, and is not very pronounced. I have made many of these centres from set-screws. Ordinary mild steel is just good enough if you do not hammer hard wood true. These seem to wear very smooth. If we had a lot of $\frac{5}{8}$-in. pins to turn we would use a $\frac{5}{8}$-in. diameter centre. Cutting pins to size is then easy. This may seem a lot of bother about lathe centres, but a happy pair of centres will help you to enjoy wood turning. No set sizes are given as lathes vary; also the work we do.

Trade lathe centres screw in, either $\frac{5}{8}$ in. or $\frac{3}{4}$ in. and I prefer this type of centre for wood-turning lathes rather than the-tapered kind. The reason is that one can unscrew a centre without hurting the bearings, and a hollow mandrel is of little use in wood-turning lathes. A four-prong chuck is useful for chair legs and similar work (see Fig. 4), and a wide two-prong chuck, called a chisel chuck, is best for turning back feet of chairs. A small chisel chuck is best for small lathes as four-prongs need more pressure from the tail-stock to make them drive. Some woods easily split if a faulty chisel chuck is used.   The driving edges should not radiate from the centre as both fangs would be in one line.   Also it is important not to have the bevel too acute so that the chuck has a splitting action.

One last word to help when you have a lot of pins to turn to one size.   You can have a tail-stock centre made to the same diameter and you have only to chisel to that size.   It avoids the unnecessary

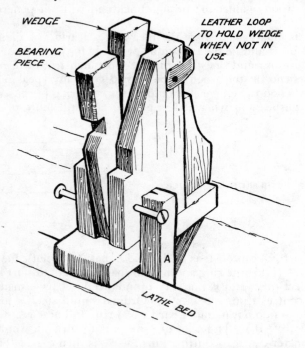

WEDGE

LEATHER LOOP
TO HOLD WEDGE
WHEN NOT IN
USE

BEARING
PIECE

A

LATHE BED

FIG. 5. BACK STEADY USED ON AN OLD LATHE.
This apparently crude device is most effective in use. It is sketched
from an old lathe in the Museum at High Wycombe, Bucks.

use of callipers.   It is a good thing to have a drill, and a centre the same size.   In practice only a few sizes are needed.

Wood steadies.   Early wood-turning for chairs was done in the forest itself on a pole or bodger's lathe around the High Wycombe district, and one is still at work there (or was when I was writing this).   In the town a treadle wheel lathe could frequently be found in a little shed at the end of the garden even within a few years back. It was hard work to treadle all day, however, and so sometimes others helped. Then steam power came, driving long lengths of shafting which worked various machines, and the chips and shavings fed the furnace, so we had cheap power. The electric motor of to-day works on a different principle, and shaving disposal is a

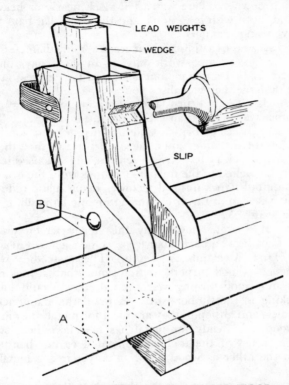

LEAD WEIGHTS

WEDGE

SLIP

B

A

FIG. 6. SIMPLE YET EFFECTIVE STEADY FOR WOOD.
The great advantage of this is that it maintains a constant light pressure.
At the same time it is positive in that it resists thrust. Furthermore
it automatically takes up to the reduced size of the wood when the
latter is turned right opposite it.

problem, but of course electricity is handy and eliminates shafting, etc. To start or stop a machine a belt was slid along from a fixed pulley to a loose pulley, an ideal system for wood-turning lathes. The modern push-button control is all right for some jobs, but it would be impossible to turn the back legs of chairs in this way as in some jobs we want a gradual start.

The old-time lathe. When you bought a lathe you had a countershaft with a three-speed cone at one end, and two pulleys about 10 in. diameter to take a 2-in. belt, one fixed to the shaft, and the other free to rotate. You bought a built-up wooden pulley to fix on to the shaft to give you the speed you wanted. The lathe had a heavy head-stock which you could only just lift, and had a central bolt hanging down. There was a tail-stock nearly as heavy, and a T rest stand, both with long bolts, and these had flat bars of iron as nuts to save using spanners.

The T rest was a casting with at least a 1-in. diameter pin, and was used for face turning work only, as in those days only chairs were made. It had a 5-h.p. motor and 10-in. centres, and if you wanted to do large diameter discs you just packed some wood under the head-stock. I could turn large table tops for letting lino in for teashop tables (far better than eating on the floor lino). The lathe beds were two pieces of British Columbian pine, and you had them planed up on the machine, and a piece sideways formed the stand at the end. Mine took 15 ft. between centres, and was used for turning newels which reached to the upstairs landings from the ground floor. We see these old lathes in local factories being made redundant by the changing design of furniture, the automatic lathe doing the mass production stuff.

Steady. But let us now study the steady which was wanted chiefly for back legs and armchair legs. One is shown in Fig. 5 and is in the High Wycombe museum. These steadies were very crudely made. Wood-turners are notoriously bad at making things. In fact, if no wood-turning was needed, they would have to go plank-stacking in the timber-yard. A few lathe manufacturers do make steadies, and although they are ideal for metal, they are of little use for wood. A steady for metal has to retain the work solidly against the thrust of the tool, and metal does not bend one way more than the other as wood does. I've yet to see metal burn as wood can.

So for wood we require a gentle thrust to counteract its tendency to bend more easily one way than the other (this is often the start of chatter in wood turning). We want a simple means of relieving this thrust when the wood starts burning; and it must have enough clearance so that a square can revolve before the wood is turned round. It must not be fussy as to size, for when we reduce the wood opposite the steady, it must adjust itself. Then, as only a few jobs require a steady, it must be easily removed from the lathe.

The wood-turner needing a steady would ask the timber-yard foreman for a chunk of throw-out wood. This he would ponder over, and at a suitable moment ask the band sawyer to saw out something as in Fig. 6. There always seemed to be a box of old bolts, and one was fitted at (A) and another (probably $\frac{1}{2}$ in.) with a wing nut on at (B). A chair-maker was enlisted to screw a block of wood on the back, and it was tried several times in the lathe to see whether the wood could revolve with it in place, and whether it would come out with the rest still in. The slip with a notch in it was pivoted at (B), and the width of wedge tried out by experiment.

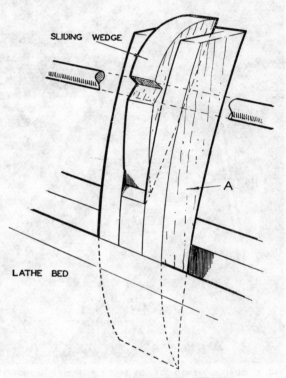

FIG. 7. SIMPLE ALTERNATIVE STEADY.
Although not so effective as the steady in Fig. 6, this has its uses for some jobs.

In the end, with the co-operation of the whole factory except the polishing shop, the job was done, a fine museum piece of work, which gladdened the heart, for it worked (that was the only reason it was made). It would help us if manufacturers would give us a start and provide the main part to fit on to the lathe bed, which is invariably round, and less handy than the two oblong sections of wood to fit it to.

Why the steady works. Let us see why it is so good. Fig. 6 shows a wedge against the underside of the lathe bed, pressing against the bolt, so forming a simple way of holding the steady firmly, yet easily removed by a biff. The wedge can be easily removed, and is to hand at the back of the steady when needed. The wood slip fits the work, and needs no special fitting. Its crudeness in no way hinders its use. If the wood becomes hot a rub with some candle-

FIG. 8. SIMPLE WOOD STEADY MADE FOR MYFORD LATHE.
The idea could be adapted to suit any make of lathe. (A) is the wedge which tends to drop down by gravity and keep the slip (B) up to the work. The slip is pivoted at (C).

grease will cure it. Should the work require more thrust, it can be given by nailing lead on to the wedge; or a rubber band can be passed over the top of the wedge and down beneath.

One man I know has a screw which grips the wedge. He pushes the wedge down and tightens the screw which holds it there. A wing nut exerts enough pressure to prevent the slip from rising or falling, but allows it to swivel by action of the wedge. Some use a wood screw, but the principle is all you need worry about. If you draw a square at centre height at your lathe bed, you can work one out for your lathe. The wedge can be quite wide as when it is withdrawn the slip goes further back out of the way. If you wish to do long stuff it is an ideal steady, and well worth making.

Alternative steady. If your lathe has twin beds you can make a simpler one which helps to steady the work, but is not as good. Still it has its uses as it can be quickly slipped into the bed where it is needed. Fig. 7 shows its principle. Part (A) slides down and so forces the slip against the work, but it does not prevent the work from moving up and down.

Perhaps you want a still simpler steady. Well, a wedge inserted between the rest and the work helps to do some jobs, but it burns easily as it has only a line contact.

Preliminary rounding. These steadies must have the work round, and back legs can be tiresome to turn round. You lightly put your hand round the revolving back leg, and, with a $\frac{3}{8}$-in. gouge, turn the part where the steady is to come. For an extremely difficult job you can rasp it round first. The hand is around the work, not so much as a steady, but to catch the job if it flies out. Remember that we are thinking of long, springy items, or they would not require a steady. If you find that it wears through to the bone, or if you can smell burning pork, try another way. Still, to put your hand around the work is helpful and safe.

CHAPTER 7 : CHUCKING JOBS

S HALL we have a few thoughts on chucking your job? A simple way of holding a bowl on a face plate is to fix it with wood screws. If a piece of baize is fixed on the bottom afterwards it hides the holes. Now, if my mother's only son had made the face plate its

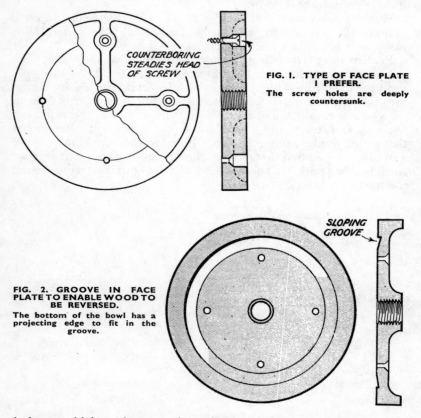

COUNTERBORING
STEADIES HEAD
OF SCREW

FIG. I. TYPE OF FACE PLATE I PREFER.
The screw holes are deeply countersunk.

FIG. 2. GROOVE IN FACE PLATE TO ENABLE WOOD TO BE REVERSED.
The bottom of the bowl has a projecting edge to fit in the groove.

SLOPING GROOVE

holes would have been made to hold a definite screw size and be deeply countersunk. The screw would remain square to the wood, because its head would fit the hole (see Fig. 1). We like short, fat screws so that we can turn the bowl thin without the screws passing right through.   I lay the baize on the bottom of the bowl, and rub the corner of the bottom of the bowl with a piece of chalk.   The size can be seen quite easily.

A bowl.   The block of wood to form a bowl has its outer side turned true to enable the inside to be hollowed out.   I have a blind friend who turns a lot of bowls, and he leaves a short pin about $\frac{3}{4}$ in. diameter on the bottom and this fits into a hole in a disc of wood. In his case this disc is fixed to the face plate proper with four wing nuts and ordinary screws hold the bowl to the disc.   This short pin he removes later with a plane which is held in his vice, and he drags the bowl across it.   There is no reason why you could not leave a pin and let it go into the face plate.   If the face plate stands out from

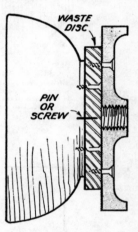

FIG. 3. WASTE DISC WITH CENTRE PIN TO
SIMPLIFY REVERSING.
The outside is turned first and a little hole made in
centre. When the wood is reversed this hole fits over
the pin.

the nose of the mandrel you could turn a shallow depression there for most likely it is threaded and so not truly circular.

One method I adopted for this reversing business was to turn a sloping groove in the face plate as in Fig. 2.   When I turned the bottom of the bowl I made the edge project to catch in it.   There is the added advantage that, should the bowl warp, this edge could be trued up on a sheet of glasspaper resting on a flat surface.

It may well be that you prefer your bowl fixed to a disc of wood (as the blind man does) and you could put a pin in this disc which would centralize the bowl, for the little hole required would be cut while turning the bottom of the bowl (see Fig. 3).

When fixing wood to the face plate if a screw seems to pull it out of truth, I ignore that screw and try another, and do this screw last.

6—P.W.T.

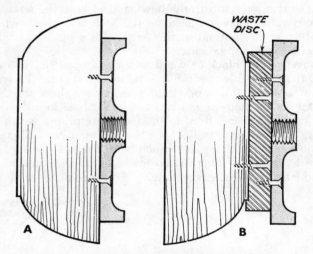

FIG. 4. ARRANGEMENT FOR REVERSING WOOD.
After turning outside as at (A) a waste block is fixed to the face plate. A recess is turned in this to receive the base of the bowl. If the face plate has a double set of holes the second set of screws can pass right through the disc into the bowl.

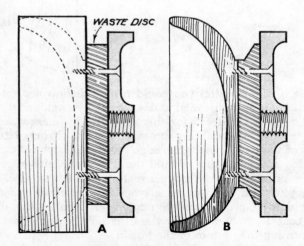

FIG. 5. TURNING WITH SINGLE CHUCKING.
Both inside and outside are turned in one operation.

It is the grain of the wood that makes the screws wander; they will find the soft spots.

Quite often a 6-in. face plate is the correct size for the bottom of the bowl, and so you can just watch that these agree. Another method is that in Fig. 4. You fix the wood to the face plate and turn the outside as at (A) the screws being near the middle where the wood is turned away later. It is removed from the face plate and a waste block screwed to the latter as at (B). A recess is turned in the waste block *exactly* to the size of the bottom of the bowl as shown, and the latter held in it with screws. Many face plates have a double set of holes, and clearance holes are bored right through the waste block to enable screws to pass through into the bowl.

Alternative chucking. Yet another plan is to turn the whole

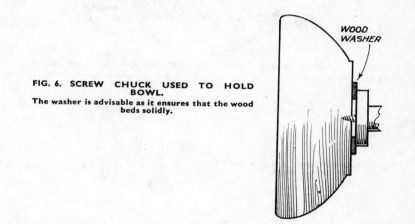

WOOD
WASHER

FIG. 6. SCREW CHUCK USED TO HOLD BOWL.
The washer is advisable as it ensures that the wood beds solidly.

bowl from one side in a single operation as in Fig. 5. The waste block has clearance holes and the fixing screws pass through both it and the face plate into the wood for the bowl. This method is handy when the wood you have is green and has to dry out. You fix the wood as at (A), rough turn it to a generous oversize, and leave to dry out for as long as possible. If you do a lot of bowls you can leave them for months. They will probably twist and shrink across the grain, and that is why you leave the wood of ample thickness. You then re-chuck as at (B) and complete the turning.

In this method you have to turn away the waste block to an extent, but this does not matter. It is also necessary when you re-chuck the wood to plane the bottom flat as it is almost sure to have twisted slightly in the drying-out process.

Those who want the best work will want no screw holes, etc., and they can glue a bottom of waste wood on the bowl and put the screws into that. It is split off when finished. As an alternative you can follow the method in Fig. 4, except that the bowl is glued into the recess with newspaper between instead of being screwed. It holds strongly for turning, but is easily prised away afterwards.

Screw chuck. Whichever way you use make sure that the bowl is firm and does not rock owing to an uneven surface as this is

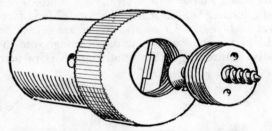

FIG. 7. SPECIAL SCREW POINT CHUCK FOR CORONET LATHE.
An ordinary wood screw is used. This avoids the fault so many screw chucks have, that of screw point breaking off.

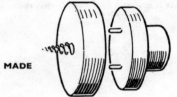

FIG. 8. SCREW POINT CHUCK MADE IN TWO PARTS.

asking for trouble. It is a good idea also to see that the rest is firm. A good central screw chuck of 3 in. diameter as in Fig. 6 can hold a 10-in. bowl easily—I have done many hundreds on one. Be sure to note how fat and short the screw is, however. A fat screw can swell the wood around it, so either use a thin ply washer between the wood and chuck face, or remove the swollen part and put the block of wood on again, testing to see that it is free from any tendency to rock. The thin washer is the better method if the wood is inclined to be a trouble to unscrew.

This is a useful chuck for turning wheels on, such as are used on toys and tea trollies, etc. as the work can be easily reversed. It is an advantage if the chuck is in two parts as in Fig. 8 as then we can use the backplate as a small face plate. We could make special discs to hold say a pot lid with a much smaller screw.

The ideal is to thread the backplate and then we have a chuck for holding egg-cups, or cruet sets absolutely rigidly with no fear of accidents such as catching the fingers on the jaws of a three-jaw chuck or the wood flying out. This chuck as shown in Fig. 9 is really the answer for school use, and could be made in the engineering department as it is only simple turning and screw cutting. It is shown in

FIG. 9. CHUCK TO HOLD WOOD FOR EGG-CUPS, ETC.
A sectional view of the chuck is given on page 92.

section in Fig. 3, page 92. I have made twenty using 26 threads per inch which could, of course, be varied. I left the bevel rough so that the wood caught in the ring and twisted it tighter. I made a bar as in Fig. 4, page 92, to undo it. I have never used it, but boys might need it.

A disc of ply as Fig. 10 might help to centralize wood on the face plate, and variations to suit your needs can be thought of. We found a disc as in Fig. 11 useful to mark the bases of floor standard or smoker's companions where the three feet came.

The holes in egg-cups are turned first, unless the chuck in Fig. 9 is used. If your lathe is true you can fix a nose piece on your screw chuck as in Fig. 12. This will drive the egg-cup block nicely between centres. The advantage of doing it this way round is that you remove the centre mark as you part the bottom off. A disadvantage is that the block might slip on the nose piece. Perhaps chalking it will help, but we put in a gramophone needle as shown. It was not seen on the finished job. You could turn half an egg and run this on the tail-stock centre as in Fig. 13. It ought to be flush with the top of the hole in the block or it will twist out.

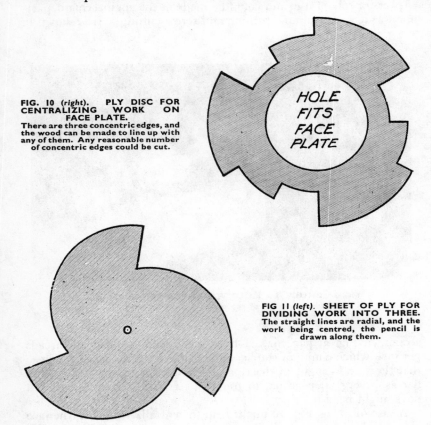

FIG. 10 (right).   PLY DISC FOR CENTRALIZING   WORK   ON FACE PLATE.
There are three concentric edges, and the wood can be made to line up with any of them. Any reasonable number of concentric edges could be cut.

HOLE
FITS
FACE
PLATE

FIG 11 (left). **SHEET OF PLY FOR DIVIDING WORK INTO THREE.** The straight lines are radial, and the work being centred, the pencil is drawn along them.

Serviette rings. These are held on a tapered mandrel as in Fig. 14. This can be chalked to give a grip, and if you leave it rough it will help to drive the ring better. You might like to use wood with the heart in it for rings as this would show a nice grain. I have done a few from an apple tree branch from my orchard. The hole must be made before it starts to split, even if it has to be trued up again after seasoning.

Fig. 15 shows a useful chuck for holding round blocks of wood when boring the holes for egg-cups or serviette rings. It can be made from a faulty piece of wood and there is no need to bore the hole smooth (which is easy). The same idea of pushing wood into a hole can be used for discs for bread-boards if care is taken not to make your cuts too heavy. If it does fly out you will not be in line of rotation and it will only be a window gone. It does save screw

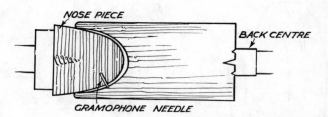

FIG. 12. NOSE PIECE ON SCREW CHUCK FOR EGG-CUPS.

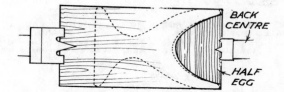

FIG. 13. ALTERNATIVE WITH NOSE ON BACK CENTRE.

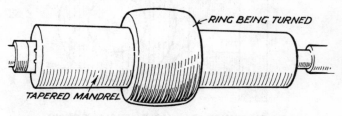

FIG. 14. TAPERED MANDREL TO HOLD SERVIETTE RINGS.

holes in the bottom of the bread-board. My men have done fancy lids, bases, and bread-boards this way, sometimes trapping a piece of garnet cloth in to give added grip.

If you wish to make the idea more complicated a tapered pin as in Fig. 16 is effective. Be sure to put in as shown as then the wood tends to tighten itself when turned. You might like to cut a groove in the wood for this to engage in. Note the direction of the grain of the wood to prevent the tapered pin from splitting it.

Back legs of chairs. Fig. 17 shows how the back legs of chairs are held. The more the pressure between centres the tighter the wedge grips. If balanced nicely quite a good speed can be used if

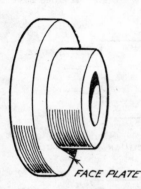

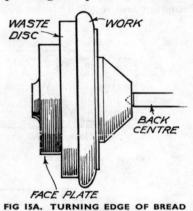

FIG. 15. SIMPLE CHUCK FOR SMALL ROUND BLOCKS.
The wood makes a friction fit in the hole.

FIG 15A. TURNING EDGE OF BREAD BOARD.
The work is held by friction between the waste disc and the cone-shaped block on the back centre.

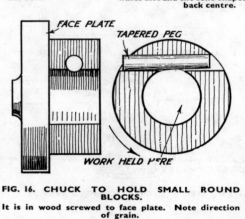

FIG. 16. CHUCK TO HOLD SMALL ROUND BLOCKS.
It is in wood screwed to face plate. Note direction of grain.

you are not nervous. A visitor at my works asked, "Do they often hit you?" and my foreman replied, "No, generally just once". The precautions to prevent that "once" are to chalk the wood and wedge to prevent it from slipping about. We have used so much chalk in

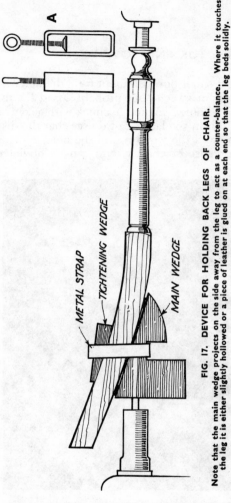

FIG. 17. DEVICE FOR HOLDING BACK LEGS OF CHAIR. Note that the main wedge projects on the side away from the leg to act as a counter-balance. Where it touches the leg it is either slightly hollowed or a piece of leather is glued on at each end so that the leg beds solidly.

High Wycombe that it's in a valley now. You can either hollow the wedge or put on pieces of thin leather as in Fig. 17 so that the ends of the driving wedge do press hard on the work. The link or strap can have a screw in as at (A) or a wedge driven in as shown in Fig. 17, but it must tighten when end pressure is put on, so it should be at a slight angle.

The main wedge is as far up the back leg as possible to shorten the distance between centres. The length of the driving centre and design of the bearings govern this. This main wedge is either loaded with lead or made much larger so that it balances the job. If held lightly between centres you can detect whether it is out of balance by the heavy part going down. Large numbers of back legs have been done in this way, but now a patent lathe is made with an extended bearing to hold the back leg at seat level, enabling them to be done at top speed.

CHAPTER 8 : TURNING BOWLS

A S an example let us take a small bowl of about 6 in. diameter by
3 in. deep, useful for nuts or sweets, but probably used for the
oddments one accumulates in a home.   A simple chuck with a central
screw would be ample to hold it in the lathe, but do see that the disc
is firm as the screw tends to swell the wood round the hole, causing
the disc to rock.   This is a cause of chatter, and can be obviated

FIG. I.   TURNING OUTSIDE OF BOWL WITH ¾-in. GOUGE.
To see the movement of the gouge turn to Figs. 3 and 4, page 84.

by the use of a ply disc as in Fig. 2, or by just removing the swelling
round the hole.

Alternatively the disc can be fixed to the face plate with screws
(see page 73).

The gouge. The outside and bottom of the bowl are done first, using a gouge. Mine is $\frac{3}{8}$ in. measured across the inside of the hollow, and is ample to take all the power a $\frac{1}{2}$-h.p. motor can give. It is a "long and strong" type of deep pattern, but this is hard to get, and expensive, and you can get on quite well without it. The term "long and strong" is a trade term for a stouter section tool than normal, and you will see why I suggest its use later on. An illustration of it appears on page 14.

Speed. "What speed do I need?" is often asked. About 1,000 r.p.m. or a speed slower than the usual speed of $\frac{1}{2}$-h.p. motors (which is about 1,400) is satisfactory. However, aim at a heavy cut at slow speed, rather than a high speed at which the tool merely brings off dust, and loses its edge. The rigidity of the lathe and its rest governs speed quite a lot.

Another question I am always asked is, "What height should the

FIG. 2. DEVICE TO PREVENT WOOD FROM ROCKING ON THE SCREW-POINT CHUCK.

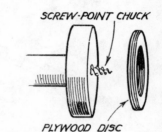

SCREW-POINT CHUCK

PLYWOOD DISC

rest be?" This does not matter much, and if you follow the instructions you will find out what suits you. Some of us are upright, some bent; lathes vary; people have their own preference in holding tools; and some like to stand with the face near to see what is happening, others well up and away from the shavings.

Cutting action of gouge. Now the following I lay great stress on. To get it right is the whole art of turning. It is "cutting wood as it prefers to be cut." When I am swanking at a demonstration, I get the tool correct, and hold the handle between two fingers, taking off long rope-like shavings that run down the hollow of the gouge. The tool does not dig in, and can use all the power with no effort on my part. If you find you have to hold the tool tightly you are probably holding it at a wrong angle to the work, so do please try to find out this straightway.

Get a cup or basin and your gouge (if anyone thinks you crackers, well don't worry; I have been so for years). Hold your basin as

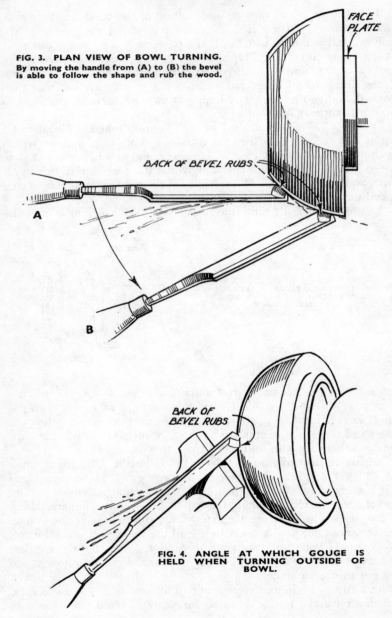

FIG. 3. PLAN VIEW OF BOWL TURNING.
By moving the handle from (A) to (B) the bevel
is able to follow the shape and rub the wood.

FACE PLATE

BACK OF BEVEL RUBS

A

B

BACK OF BEVEL RUBS

FIG. 4. ANGLE AT WHICH GOUGE IS HELD WHEN TURNING OUTSIDE OF BOWL.

though you were turning it and hold your gouge slightly on its side,
but with its short ground bevel rubbing the cup.   Fig. 3 will help
you to see what I mean.   Move the tool from (A) to (B), and you
will notice that the end of the handle moves through quite a distance.
You govern the shape of the bowl by how you move the end of the
handle.   Perhaps you can picture yourself taking a heavier or lighter
cut by adjusting the bevel to the work.

The tool points upwards as in Figs. 1 and 4, and you will see
now the most suitable height of rest for you.   Possibly the lathe bed
may get in the way, but you will find you can get over this trouble
in practice.

Sharpening angle of gouge.   Now gouges for face plate turning
are best ground square across and at the angle shown in Fig. 5
(about 45°), not as you buy them, which is far too long a bevel (don't

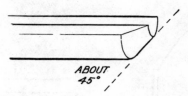

ABOUT
45°

FIG. 5. SHARPENING ANGLE OF GOUGE.

ask me why they do it).   You may think that the corners will dig
in, but in practice they do not.   I suggest that you hold the gouge
to the cup again.   If your gouge has too long a bevel it has to be
pointed upwards at such an angle that it is not possible to use the
rubbing effect of its bevel to avoid its digging into the work.

Also, if the tool is ground to a nose point instead of straight across,
you will notice that the cutting edge recedes from the work just
where you want it to cut, which is from the centre of the gouge to
one side.

The bottom of the bowl must be finished as it is not possible to
work on it again.   It should be slightly hollow.   One other point;
before you take it from the lathe make a little centre hole to go on to
the chuck when it is reversed.   If, however, you are using the face
plate rather than the screw point chuck this is unnecessary.

I have drawn the shape I like in Fig. 6, but it is a free country so
you can do your own design.   Between you and me, however, a
shape that is not drawn with compasses does not show up if it is
not nicely true.   If you doubt this try turning a ball.

Hollowing.   The block is now on the chuck for hollowing out,

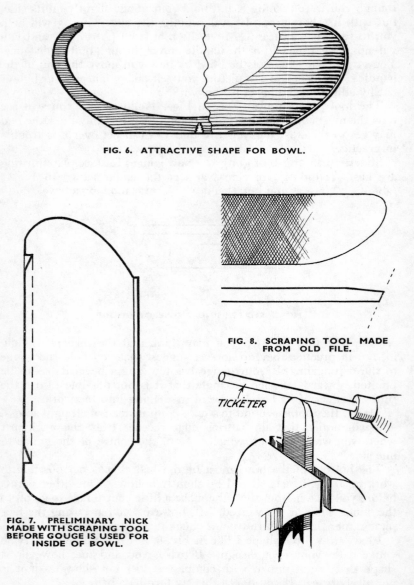

FIG. 6. ATTRACTIVE SHAPE FOR BOWL.

FIG. 8. SCRAPING TOOL MADE
FROM OLD FILE.

TICKETER

FIG. 7. PRELIMINARY NICK
MADE WITH SCRAPING TOOL
BEFORE GOUGE IS USED FOR
INSIDE OF BOWL.

FIG. 9. TURNING EDGE OF SCRAP-
ING TOOL WITH TICKETER.

nice and firm owing to the slightly hollow surface. In the case of face plate fixing remember to use short screws; otherwise they will project through the bottom of the bowl and leave unsightly marks, to say nothing of knocking the edge off the turning tool. First make a groove near the edge of the bowl as in Fig. 7. This is to prevent the gouge from sliding across as it is started. It is formed by using the chisel flat on the rest. You cannot have the bevel of the tool rubbing until it has something to rub on, and this groove provides a rubbing surface for it.

The same principle is employed in using the gouge inside as described in turning the outside; keep the bevel rubbing. If in your design there is a flat part at the bottom of the bowl, hold the tool near the rest and slide your hand along. Fig. 6, page 19 is a view of the bowl from above showing how the gouge is used with its bevel rubbing.

Scraping rather than cutting. I now describe a tool which calls for entirely different treatment, so do not apply the same methods as those just described.

Many like this tool as it has no funny ways, and requires little skill in its use. However, it needs skill in getting a good edge on it, and in finding suitable steel. A file is generally all right, but not so satisfactory as an old mortise chisel. Fig. 8 shows how to grind it. Note that the curve as shown is more useful than if it is just a half-round. The side view shows the angle at which it is ground. Note that the top surface is ground well away as the middle of the file is softer and better for use.

There are two ways of sharpening it after grinding to shape. One way is simply to give it a *few* rubs with a coarse stone on the bevel to leave a burr on the face or top surface. For some woods it can be used direct from the grindstone, in which case the edge is always ground *after* the top serrations have been ground away. This kind of sharpening is best for elm, oak, and poor mahogany as the burr grips the fibres, and removes them. For walnut, beech, or similar woods an edge put on with a ticketer is better as this cuts it cleanly. As a comparison think of a bread knife with its notches cutting bread, and a ham knife cutting slices of ham. (I won't suggest that you cut up the ham now as we must get on with our bowl.)

To those not familiar with a "ticketer", it is only a hard steel rod. The tool is first given a fine edge with an oil stone. Mine is a hone as used by barbers and cost £5, but any fine stone is satisfactory. The ticketer is rubbed across the top face of the tool with pressure at the edge rather, evenly all over. Then two or three rubs on the bevel, again towards the edge, will put a good edge on the tool as shown in Fig. 9.   Cabinet-makers use the ticketer when sharpening a scraper for cleaning up veneers, etc.   The turned-up edge for turning is similar.

Hunting for steel and experimenting on sharpening these scraping tools can be most interesting.   Many turners prefer them entirely for face turning as they cut the parts of work which are against the grain better then gouges do.   Of course, we never finish off with a gouge—unless we wish work to be entirely hand-turned.   The

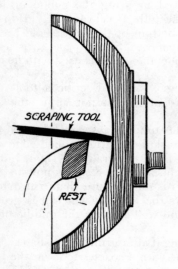

SCRAPING TOOL

REST

FIG. 10. FINISHING INSIDE OF BOWL WITH SCRAPING TOOL.
When the grain runs across as here only fine cuts should be made, specially for final cuts.

scraper tool points slightly downwards from the rest, which is about centre height, see Fig. 10.   If you point it upwards it will dig in badly and may break the tool.   Try to take a shaving off rather than just let the tool rub the work as the edge soon goes off if it only rubs the work.

There is little more to add in using these tools, but to get the "feel" of them try the rest a little away from the work, and you will feel a nice bite when the sharpening angle of tool is right and the angle you are holding it is correct.   When you have mastered it, long ribbons of shavings will go over your head, and you will get the thrill of craftsmanship.

To finish off the surface should be glasspapered.   The thin edge especially is best done with glasspaper; fibres are inclined to break out if turned.   Let the paper trail in the direction of rotation or it may double your fingers back. Too high a speed will burn them, too, so I do urge you not to rely on glasspaper to do the job of turning. Rather try to turn your bowl cleanly. It always seems to look much better if turned without a lot of papering. Few woods need no glasspapering, however; the smoother the surface the better the polish.

Wet wood. Sometimes you will have wood for turning which is not dry. As wood for bowls is invariably thick it takes a long time to dry out naturally. In this case the best plan is to rough turn the wood whilst it is wet, and then set it aside for as long as possible to dry before finishing it off. The hollowing-out speeds up the drying considerably. When you come to finish it off you will probably find

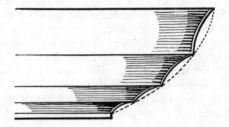

FIG. II. HOW BOWL WITH HOLLOWS FOLLOWS
SWEEPING CURVE.

that it has become oval and most likely twisted. Run a plane over the bottom to level it before re-chucking it. It is of course necessary to leave the bowl very full in size when rough turning, as otherwise there will not be enough wood left for the finished shape.

In Fig. 11 is a bowl design with a series of shallow hollows on the outside. Note, however, that the general line of the bowl follows a sweeping curve as shown by the dotted line. Pencil lines are marked on the revolving bowl at the ridges, and the hollows formed with a rounded scraping tool.

Incidentally in any bowl in which the grain runs across there will be two places in which the grain is liable to tear out (the idea is shown clearly in Fig. 8, page 146). The remedy is to keep the scraping tool sharp and remove only fine finishing cuts. In this way all roughness can be taken out.

Small flexible hand scrapers shaped with a curved end are extremely useful for troublesome places. They are used with the work still (not revolving).

7—P.W.T.

CHAPTER 9 : SPECIAL JOBS—EGG-CUPS, SERVIETTE RINGS, CABRIOLE LEGS, AND BALLS

THE purpose of this chapter is not so much to give designs as to discuss the problems involved in their turning and to see how to overcome them. When you have a number of similar items to turn you soon learn to devise methods of doing the work well and quickly.

EGG-CUPS

Holding the wood. Now from long experience I am sure that it is advisable to bore the hole first, or, at least, only to round the blocks before finishing the outside. The holding of the blocks firm in the lathe is really the trouble, as turning the hollow involves rather a wide cut. You may have a three-jaw chuck such as engineers use, and if you turn a little rim on the end of the block to catch in the little hollow in the corner of the jaws, they will be held quite firmly. In fact using this method I recently turned a large hole 12 in. long in a piece of cherry to hold a scroll to present to Her Majesty the Queen. A three-jaw chuck is not often found in a wood-

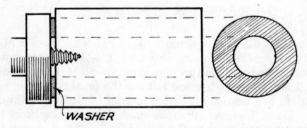

FIG. I. SCREW CHUCK WITH WASHER FOR EGG-CUP.

turner's kit, however, as its jaws can injure you. In any case it soon becomes clogged with dust, so do not shout up the chimney for one at Christmas.

Some hold the block on the screw chuck, and, as egg-cups are turned in a close-grained wood, it is often successful. Be sure they do not rock, however. The trouble is that screws do not hold well in end grain wood, so rather than screw up too tight put a washer behind the block as in Fig. 1. This will also avoid rocking. A better way is to bore a hole in a thick piece of wood fixed to the face-plate to take the blocks after they have been rounded to size. Do not bore the hole too smooth (this should be easy), and take care that the blocks fit, especially at the front end, or they will come out. The blocks are driven into the hole, and either an oblique hole or a hole in the middle, if your lathe mandrel is hollow, will enable you to poke them out with a rod when finished.

A useful form of screw chuck in which an ordinary wood screw is used is shown on page 76. The weakest part of a screw chuck is that the screw is liable to snap off with continued use. Any size of ordinary countersunk screw within the limits of the chuck can be used.

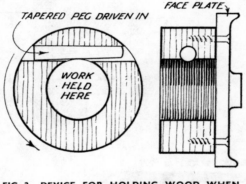

FIG. 2. DEVICE FOR HOLDING WOOD WHEN TURNING.

Wood chuck. If you delight in and enjoy making something complicated, a taper pin driven in as in Fig. 2 holds the work firmly, and is on the same principle as the fixing of bicycle pedal cranks. It is advisable to use a large-diameter block so that the pin does not protrude, and note that the pin goes in away from you when the hole is above centre. This is because the wood will tend to pull it in more as you turn. The hole is across the grain, or you might split the block. If you are still not satisfied turn a little groove in the egg-cup block where the taper pin goes.

Special chuck. I have left the best way of holding blocks until the last, but it requires an engineer's lathe to make it (see Fig. 3). It is described because many schools have a metal lathe, and some wood turners have friends. One advantage is that there is no need for great accuracy in rounding the blocks, and although a bevelled part is left on the block this bevel need not be continuous if the size

does not allow it.   Another good point is that there are no dangerous
projections; the whole thing is quite smooth, so school teachers will
sleep better at night.   The whole of the egg-cup can be turned,
inside and out, but it does waste a short piece in the chuck.   The
many chucks I have made have 26 threads per inch, and I mention
this because it has proved satisfactory in use.   A fine thread holds
tighter than a coarse one.   If you are worried about undoing it, a
tool as Fig. 4 will grip it well, though I have found the one I made
not wanted.   Still the idea may help in removing things, say, from a
screw chuck that have got too tight to remove with the hands alone.

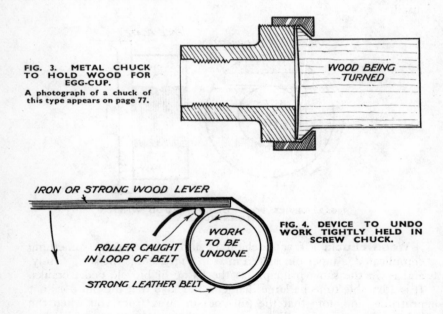

FIG. 3.   METAL CHUCK
TO HOLD WOOD FOR
EGG-CUP.
A photograph of a chuck of
this type appears on page 77.

WOOD BEING
TURNED

IRON OR STRONG WOOD LEVER

ROLLER CAUGHT
IN LOOP OF BELT

WORK
TO BE
UNDONE

STRONG LEATHER BELT

FIG. 4. DEVICE TO UNDO
WORK TIGHTLY HELD IN
SCREW CHUCK.

The wood is roughly turned to the required shape between centres
first.
    Hollowing out.   Our wood ought to be held firmly now by one
of the methods, so we will hollow it out, a quite simple matter.
A turner was giving a demonstration and used a special rest fitted
with a handle.   This was placed on the rest proper, and used to
support the tool which was held in the other hand.   But at his works
he did not do it that way.   You do not need anything so elaborate.
A scraper tool, made from an old file a little smaller profile than an

egg is what you require; that shown in Fig. 5 would be ideal as we are dealing with close-grained wood.

I would like you to follow closely the following as it is quite possible to rake out the wood and leave a poor finish if you do not understand the principle. Now it is a fact that a gentleman once gave me a first-class lathe for saying "Don't turn the taper on that leg from the small diameter end; you would not sharpen a pencil that way." The idea is so simple that it seems silly to mention it, but in fact this very principle of cutting wood the way a pencil is sharpened is extremely important. *"Cutting wood as it prefers to be cut"* I call it, and in spindle turning it means always cutting from larger diameter to smaller.

To get the same effect in our hole in the egg-cup we must start in the middle at the bottom, and work outwards. I think that is clear.

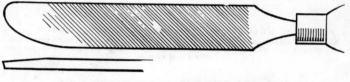

FIG. 5. SCRAPING TOOL MADE FROM OLD FILE.

In sharpening a pencil we probably hold the knife at an angle so that it slices rather than cuts squarely across. A paring cut is much nicer, and the same effect is got by holding the chisel at an angle in spindle work. To get this paring action in our hole we must point the tool upwards so that the point of the tool is higher, or we can lift the right-hand side of the tool from the rest which has a similar effect. If you do this you will get a cleaner cut.

It may be that your lathe is rather light and chatters. Well it helps if the right-hand side of the cutter rubs the work as it comes up. The idea is shown in Fig. 6. In fact many tools use this action for doing long holes 6 ft. long and 3 in. diameter in textile rollers and holes in ships' metal shafts, so it may help you in some of your turning problems. Many use a small gouge for doing this hollow in egg-cups, but its cutting action is wrong as we ought to start at the bottom and come out. Try it, and you may succeed as it is a nice piece of work, but it requires skill, and for that reason I say "Try it".

Egg-cups are usually done in sets, and a drill helps some people to get them all the same depth. I am thinking of a large drill held in tail-stock chuck, and just a pencil mark on it as in Fig. 7. The drill

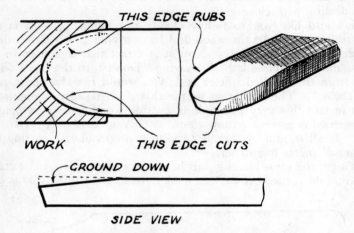

FIG. 6. HOLLOWING TOOL FOR INSIDE OF EGG-CUP.
An old file makes an excellent tool for this work. In use one edge cuts while
the other rubs. Note that the upper face is ground down in order to use the
file's soft centre.

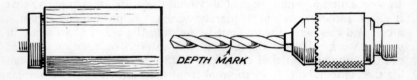

FIG. 7. PRELIMINARY HOLE BEING DRILLED.

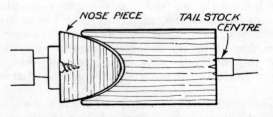

**FIG. 8. WOOD HELD ON HALF-EGG ATTACHED TO
NOSE PIECE.**

is stationary, and the mark lasts quite a time in showing how deep to bore the hole. The diameter of the hole can be checked with dividers, taking care that the point bears on the rest near to you before you let it touch the work (see Fig. 9). Generally we prefer a pencil mark and a piece of card or ply, as dividers are liable to shift. If you must have a template for the shape of the hole, well do so, but it is quite unnecessary. If you use an actual egg as the lathe is going, please let me know how you get on, but do not send the results.

While we are doing the hole it is helpful to do the top, either square across or with a small radius according to the design. With just a rub of paper we then finish our hole.

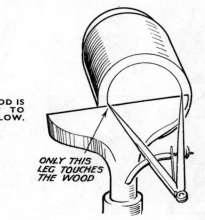

FIG. 9. HOW END OF WOOD IS MARKED WITH DIVIDERS TO SHOW EXTENT OF HOLLOW.

ONLY THIS
LEG TOUCHES
THE WOOD

Turning the outside. Now we will mount the block to finish off the outside, and if your lathe runs truly, that is the two centres are in line, I recommend that you turn a nose piece fixed on your screw chuck, like half an egg only longer. Your hole will fix on that, and the tail-stock centre will push against the bottom of the egg-cup as in Fig. 8. Thus it will be easy to cut the bottom of the egg-cup cleanly down. If you are worried by the half-egg of wood not driving the work, rub a little chalk on it. At the factory we put a little nail in it, and filed it to a point. It may be of interest to you that our ring centre in the tail-stock for turning egg-cups was less than ¼ in. diameter and so did not absorb much power.

If your lathe is not quite true, turn half an egg or less so that it fits the hole in the block and is about flush with top of the egg-cup. You must make it a nice fit. If too long it will not be firm when you start turning. Let this half-egg run on the tail-stock centre, and oil it well to prevent it from burning on the centre.   Sometimes chalking will stop it moving about in its hole.

Designs.   Now comes the great moment when we turn it to our own design, and I am sure your first attempts will be quite exclusive. Please do not think I am disparaging your work as many amateurs

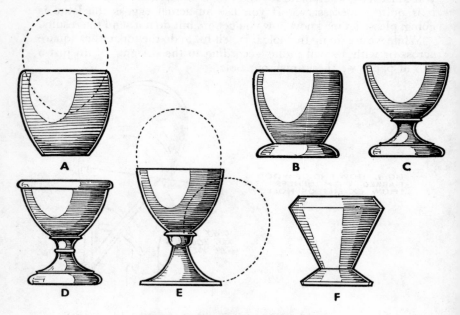

FIG. 10. SIX DESIGNS FOR EGG-CUPS.
A stand with recesses to hold egg-cups could also be turned.

do extremely fine work, and I am trying to help.   Someone once said "there should be nothing in a design without a reason for it". Well (A) Fig. 10 suits that all right, and, as we always steady an egg-cup in use, it would be quite satisfactory.   It is similar to a *Virol* jar which was designed by a famous man, but a foot will help to make it more steady so (B) will provide that.   Tradition seems to want a small neck such as those on china cups and wine glasses, so here is health to (C).   For some reason necks always look best thin, and then we find we must put something round them to make them larger.   So we will copy the architect when he wants to make a pillar look fatter (D).

Art students are fond of designing around imaginary circles, and can create a cat, or bird using circles and ovals to start off with. Using a couple of eggs (E) is the result. Some may see a modern look in (F), though the artist may well say that it is hopeless to ask a hen to lay an egg to suit it. Incidentally straight lines in turning are best if curved a little (if you know what I mean); concave to give

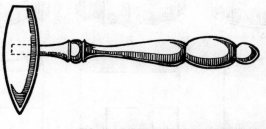

FIG. 11. MINIATURE MALLET FOR CRACKING EGGS
These are quite unnecessary but they make a turning job.

a lighter look and convex to give a heavier look. A long parallel spindle is inclined to look hollow. We could go on with these designs indefinitely but it does seem that the simpler designs look best. Of course, if you like your eggs fried you won't need a design for our egg-cup at all.

Mallets. Mallets are a luxury at the table. Although their use is to break the egg with, other means are just as effective. But perhaps a little game of table croquet or golf will liven the meal up. I have only drawn one (Fig. 11), but I think it is worth while in a happy household to have some.

SERVIETTE RINGS

The same system of holding the wood for doing the hole in our egg-cups is used except, of course, that we bore a plain hole. Fig. 12 gives several designs. It is good practice to see how cleanly we can bore this hole by holding the tool so that it pares the wood out. If we hold it level the fibres of wood will tend to be raked out, and the tool tends to chatter as well. To do the outside of the ring we just drive it on to a slightly tapered piece of wood held between centres, and chalk it should it tend to slip (Fig. 13).

You may have some wood perhaps with the heart in it, and normally it would split as it dries if turned into, say, a leg. It is quite all right for serviette rings providing that it is not split already. If it is green wood (unseasoned) bore it out, and leave it for a time. Wood

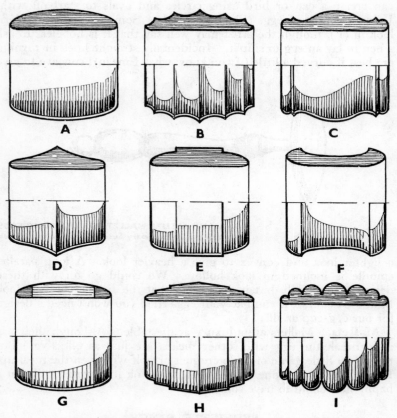

FIG. 12. DESIGNS FOR SERVIETTE RINGS IN PART SECTION

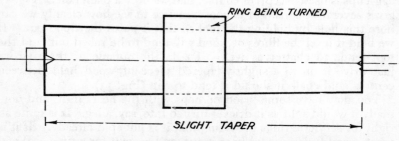

FIG. 13. WOOD FOR SERVIETTE RINGS HELD ON TAPERED PIECE.

turned this way has a nice grain which we cannot have in other articles because it will split. There is a famous college near Windsor that complained that my serviette rings were not thick enough, for in throwing them about at the table they break. Well they evidently have their use, but on this score I am in favour of mallets as well.

FIG. 14. SET OF RINGS BUILT UP IN TWO WOODS.
These rings were turned by E. C. Elstree-Wilson to whom we are indebted for this photograph.

There is just one point in boring the hole in the mallet and similar jobs. The drill will wander unless you bore it across the layers of grain (which is best) or with them. There are I know bits such as the *Forstner* which bore nicely in any direction, but are not often found, so if you put a little point on your twist drill when you grind it you won't have so much trouble in drilling wood true.

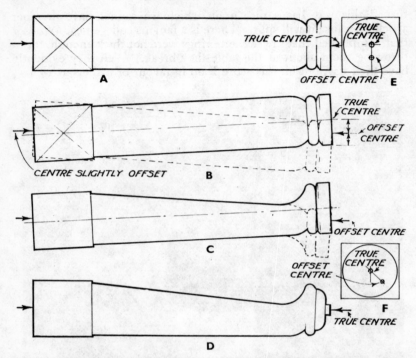

FIG. 15.   A. Both ends at true centre, and wood turned to a cylinder except the square.   B. Wood offset at tailstock midway between true centre and edge of wood. Headstock end slightly offset other way.   C. Wood turned down to taper in line with "cone" (see Fig. 16). D. Wood back at true centre and toe turned.   E. Direction of offsetting for round table. F. Direction of offsetting for square stool.

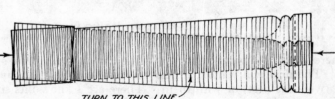

TURN TO THIS LINE

FIG. 16. HOW "CONE" APPEARS ON REVOLVING WOOD.
The wood is turned down to the dotted line including the hollow at the foot.

CABRIOLE LEG

We come now to a leg much in favour for stools, and easy to do. Its top part ought to be shaped by hand, but we are wood turners. You can, of course, do it all complete with corner pieces, and only turn the toe, which is very helpful.   Incidentally we earned 12s. an hour doing these toes at 1½d. each, but there was never enough of them.   The first thing is to turn the leg as in Fig. 15A, and then to put it out of truth (B) about half way between the true centre and the

FIG. 17. PHOTOGRAPH OF CABRIOLE LEG BEING TURNED.
This shows how the wood is offset at the centres.

outside edge.   For round stools or coffee tables it is out of true towards one side (E), but for square stools towards a corner (F).   If we did it to a corner in a round stool it would appear to be marching round.   It shows a finer sense of observation if we make the grain of the wood follow the leg.   Few squares of wood have the grain running straight down them.   Fig. 17 shows the work in the lathe.

As the wood revolves we can see the bead; also the outline of a cone. The latter appears solid, whilst the rest can be partly seen through as it revolves as shown in Fig. 16.   With a large gouge we turn away the leg to the cone just avoiding touching the bead.   The gouge is not twisted as is usual in using gouges, but if you use a small gouge twist it as you do hollows in a normal way.   The gouge is ¾ in. ground squarely across, and so the shavings come off from different parts as we move it round the hollow, taking care we just let the bevel rub in the hollow.   The gouge is right for sliding down the leg, too, but is followed by a fine cut with the chisel.

The little bead at the ankle on page 28 is not usual; in fact it weakens the leg, but it looks nice. The top of the leg has to be knocked true so as to have full diameter near the bead.   Glasspaper

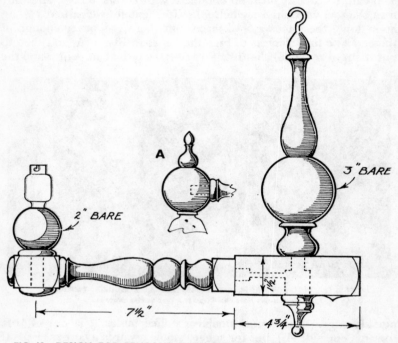

FIG. 18. DESIGN FOR PENDANT WITH EITHER THREE OR FOUR ARMS.
If the hanging type of lamp and shade is preferred the detail at A can be followed.

is a useful stuff for turners, although I have not used it for many years.   It will soften the unevenness caused where true centre meets out of centre at the top of the leg.   (In High Wycombe we use partly worn garnet cloth and paper from the furniture firms.)   Now we set the leg to run on its true centre and round the bottom of the leg (Fig. 15D).   This prevents weakness in the toe; it also is nicer to move about on carpets, etc.

BALLS

The pendant in Fig. 18 is given, not so much as a design, but because it exemplifies some interesting work in turning, notably in ball turning.

Turning balls. All sorts of things in art are repeated, music especially, and it does seem to show a pattern. In this design it is a ball, or rather ten of them. The finer points to remember in the design are that balls are best done *round*. It is quite an art, and makes you feel proud when you have done one. (Quite honestly I do too, but I usually used to avoid them when I was an employer.)

To make a good job of turning balls, calliper the diameter of the wood as turned, and measure along the same length. Cut down, using either a $\frac{1}{4}$-in. chisel or the corner of the long cornered chisel. We have now the diameter and length right as in Fig. 19.

In large balls use the small gouge. Other balls are best done

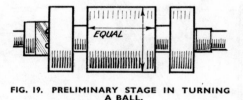

FIG. 19. PRELIMINARY STAGE IN TURNING
A BALL.

using a $\frac{1}{2}$-in. chisel ground square across, but any size *would* do it. The gouge, say $\frac{3}{8}$-in. half-round, is started square to the work, with the underneath bevel touching as at (A), Fig. 20. The rest is not too near. The handle moves to left and the cutting edge goes to the right (B and C). It does not slide along the rest as it does this right-hand half of the ball. The handle is also lifted in a circular motion as Fig. 20 shows. Note how the tool swivels on the rest, and is twisted too as it goes over. The height of the rest does not matter; just suit yourself, but if too near the work it makes the movement too severe to control. The underneath bevel rubs the work and does not dig in if you observe this rule. Generally turners do not work on top of the work enough. The gouge will not do a clean corner, but this is easy to correct with the point of the long-cornered chisel.

For smaller balls I suggested a chisel ground square across, and the reason is that it avoids having two goes at it. The heel of the long-cornered chisel is best for doing gentle curves, but the point for when you get more round the curve. Therefore you have to twist the chisel over in doing a ball, but if you use one ground square across the job is done in one movement. The difficulty is the start on top of the ball, but if you use the right-hand corner of the tool and rest the bevel of the chisel on top of the wood (which means keeping the handle end low) all will be well. The handle is to the left which gives the tool a paring action same as a long-cornered chisel would do.

The above is for the right-hand half of the ball, and you can easily follow it for the other half. The handle is moved in a rising circular movement, and it is this that governs the shape of the ball. You can take it from me that wood-turners detest ball designs, but feel proud when they do them nicely, which is true craftsmanship. There is far more joy in mastering something difficult than dodging

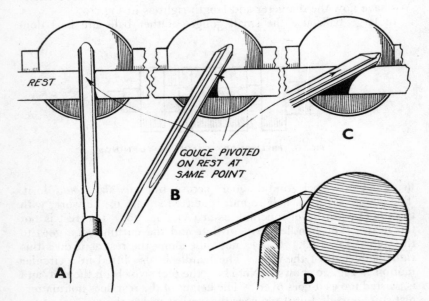

FIG. 20. HOW BALL IS TURNED USING THE ⅜-in. GOUGE.
Start the cut as at A, and, pivoting the gouge on the rest, move handle to the left as at B and C, twisting the gouge over on to its side. D is a side view.

round it and introducing something else, so get some scrap wood, and try doing a few balls as practice.

Angle of tools. The fault of many wood-turners is that they hold the tools far too tightly and try to force them around, whereas a gentle touch is much more likely to produce good work. The angle at which a tool is held is well worth a careful study. If correct the tool will not dig in, and you will enjoy a thrill that only the true craftsman can have. If the job, whatever it is, need not be done well, need it be done at all? I would like you to think on this point as too many never strive for perfection. They themselves suffer, and never enjoy the thrill of successful accomplishment that could be theirs.

It is odd that I am explaining how to do a ball as I generally recommend avoiding curves that can be done with compasses, but a ball is the only shape that looks the same from all angles. Now the upright part in Fig. 18 has not quite the same outline as the arms, because we look at it from a low angle. It therefore has the neck longer, and thinner as shown.

Centre boss. The central boss can be square, or round having four or three arms, just as you like. It is $4\frac{3}{4}$ in. across and, as it has to be mounted on the face plate to recess it for the wires, you may as well turn it as shown.

Holes. The holes and pins can be a headache when it comes to

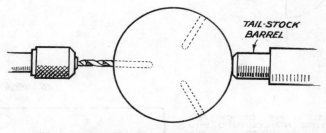

TAIL-STOCK BARREL

FIG. 21. HOW HOLES IN THE BALL ARE DRILLED.
The centre is removed from the tailstock.

fixing it all up, and care taken here is well repaid. The holes are best done first as the drill governs their size and this in turn governs the pin size. We used Russell Jennings bits just the same as cabinet-makers use. Ask for "dowel" bits as they are shorter. They are also made for machine use with a parallel shank if you like, but we used to cut off the square from the hand-brace type.

We mark where the holes are to go in our central boss, then with a $\frac{1}{8}$ in. or just over ordinary twist drill bore the holes. In the square design we use the tail-stock centre to push the wood against the drill held in the chuck. For the round boss which has three holes we take the centre out and let the tail-stock barrel push the wood as in Fig. 21. If you wish you can, when in a little way, let the wood rotate on the drill. If the rest is near you can see if the hole is going towards the centre of the boss by noting how near each side is to the rest. We just let the wood spin, and if out we push the wood with a bias to correct the error (it can break the drill). The

8—P.W.T.

trouble is that wood can be bored truly with the grain or across it, but with three radial holes we just cannot do it, so sometimes you must bore the holes and allow for the drill to wander in the bias you put so that the hole is really where you want it.

Useful template. If you are likely to want several things with three holes in them such as bases, etc., which would always stay level (whereas four feet might not) it is a good plan to make a template as shown in Fig. 22. Ours had an inch hole in it, and we just

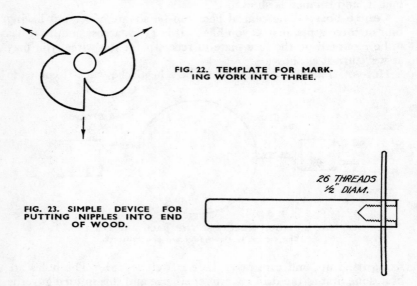

FIG. 22. TEMPLATE FOR MARK-
ING WORK INTO THREE.

FIG. 23. SIMPLE DEVICE FOR
PUTTING NIPPLES INTO END
OF WOOD.

26 THREADS
½" DIAM.

laid it on the wood and drew lines where the arrows are. It proved very useful.

Sizes of holes. We now have $\frac{1}{8}$-in. holes in our boss. The point of the bit will follow these holes, but we have to push the blocks using the tail-stock as before. You can remove the thread on the point of bit. We left ours on, but don't try to bore holes without the pilot hole if you do leave the thread on centre of the bit. It will only pull into the wood. The correct point is a pyramid for fast rotating machine bits. The sizes of holes we used were: central one for column $\frac{3}{4}$ in., but we threaded that one; $\frac{3}{4}$ in. plain hole for arms; $\frac{5}{8}$ in. for lamp ball which had $\frac{1}{4}$ in. hole for wire, but $\frac{5}{16}$ in. for the brass nipple in its top. These nipples have $\frac{3}{8}$ in. coarse Whit. thread which screws nicely into a $\frac{5}{16}$ in. hole. The lamp holder is $\frac{1}{2}$ in. by 26 threads same as $\frac{1}{2}$ in. brass thread, but other sorts of nipples are available.   The hole for wire in arms was $\frac{5}{16}$ in. and also in column, but this also had a nipple.   A hook was screwed on here to hang it up by.   Some of these hooks have the screw in them. Their use does give that professional look to the job.

In some houses the electric bulbs are too near the ceiling.   They can hang down instead of being on top.   In this case the arm can end in a pin, say $\frac{5}{8}$ in., and go into a ball as in Fig. 18 (A).   We did the holes in the arms in rather a dangerous way.   First we drilled a $\frac{5}{16}$ in. hole using a drill in the lathe and pushed the wood on to it. When in a little way we let the wood revolve and could then easily centralize it if out.   We had now a hole which was, we hoped, in the right direction and we put a special shell auger in the lathe, letting it stick out about $8\frac{1}{2}$ in. so that it just met the hole drilled across end of arm.   The dangerous part was that it could come out in the neck, so we avoided putting our fingers there.   These shell augers will drill long true holes when the wood revolves and the augur is stationary, but it is hardly worthwhile to do it for these arms.

The cross hole in the arm for the lamp holder is bored $\frac{1}{8}$ in., then the $\frac{5}{8}$ in. dowel bit, Russell Jennings pattern, is put in the chuck of the lathe and the tail-stock, with no centre in it, brought to bear against it.   The hole is bored from both sides to save splitting out the wood.   If your bit has been sharpened badly (by someone else), that is, if the fangs have been sharpened from outside, it will split the arms.

Special device for nipples.   Now, if you are going to do electric woodware in a serious way you soon find nipples for lamp holders can be troublesome to screw in, and get all cockeyed.   So I suggest you get an old brass lamp holder or anything with a $\frac{1}{2}$ in. brass thread (26 threads per inch) in it, and make a tool, fixing it into a suitable handle.   I've made quite a lot of them for my friends as in Fig. 23, and, like me, it's darned simple but it works.   You screw the nipple into it, then screw the nipple into the wood.   You can see how true you are doing that by looking at the handle.   The handle is now unscrewed from the nipple, but, by the way of things in this world, out comes the nipple from the wood.   In fact, however, it does not do so for the pin is pulled out of the tool and so the thread is quite free in the tool.   The cross handle helps you to twist the tool easily. It is well worth making if you propose to do much in this line.

Our factory had a lot of various special things and we knew where to find them.   As you accumulate them I do suggest drawers, boxes, etc., to keep them in for shavings do hide things so easily in a turning shop.

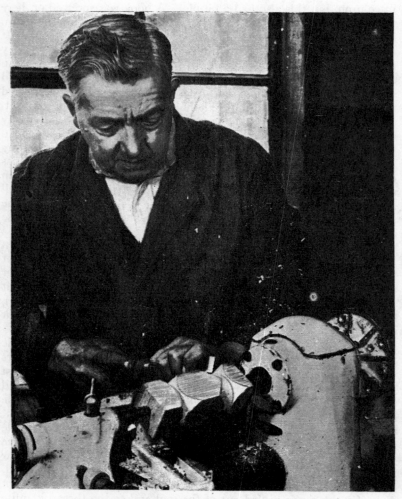

CUTTING CURVED SHOULDER WITH THE CHISEL.
This shows the second cut being made after the waste has been cleared away.

CHAPTER 10 : CUTTING DOWN SQUARES, TURNING PINS, PARTING, HOLLOWS

I NOW describe the use of the 1½-in. long-cornered chisel in cutting down squares or pummels such as in chair legs.

Cutting down squares. Nearly all legs which are used in tables, stands, chairs, and stools have them. The square of wood from which the leg is turned is left untouched locally to enable mortises or dowel holes to be cut. It is easy enough to turn the wood between the squares with gouge and chisel. The problem is in finishing up to the square. Sometimes the finish is straight across as at A, Fig. 1. In other cases it is rounded or of serpentine shape (B and C).

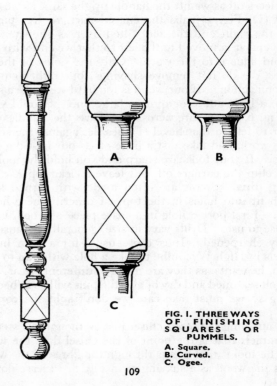

FIG. 1. THREE WAYS
OF FINISHING
SQUARES OR
PUMMELS.
A. Square.
B. Curved.
C. Ogee.

Only one end is described as the other end is cut in the same way, but the other way round.   Fig. 2 shows what we are trying to do. In turning we mark a cross on the parts of the wood to be left square. We first hold the long-cornered chisel over the work on its edge, and, as we lift the handle, down goes the point of the chisel into the square.   It is shown away from the wood in Fig. 3 for clearness. We have a part of the square cut away in triangular shavings as shown. The handle of the tool is held to the left so that bevel (A) is in line with the cut across the work.   If the tool were held square to the work it would rub at an obtuse angle.   The bevel of the tool (B) which is underneath rubs the work and prevents digging in.   As the tool penetrates we tip part (C) over to right a little, as the shavings might get larger than we can manage.   We go in until we get a continuous line round the work.   Note that we *lift the handle* end, not push it in.

The next operation is to point the tool where the curve starts, and split pieces off as we lift the handle up the same as we did before. The bevel (D, Fig. 5) rubs the curved part, so we start with the handle to the right and the tool tilted over as shown.   As we lift the handle end it is moved to the left so that we end with the tool on its edge and square to the work.   Only the point of the tool does any work.   We do not remove shavings, but rather cut the wood with splitting action.   If our wood is too hard we make a second cut. We can do a little curve or quite a large one.   Should your design be as in Fig. 6, cut square across, we have the handle end of the chisel over to left so that bevel (E) lies flat against the square to be left on the work, and take just a little off as our first dig in leaves it rather sore.   If your tools are sharp and you hold the tool as shown, it will not chip the corners off, but leave a clean job.

Turning pins.   Stools are often made with turned legs having pins which fit into holes in the top.   I describe here how to turn these pins.   First bore a hole in a spare piece of wood using the bit you propose to use.   Drills vary in size, generally because they have been badly sharpened.   It is quite usual for a man buying, say, $\frac{3}{8}$-in. dowels in High Wycombe to take a hole with him to show what size of $\frac{3}{8}$ in. he wants, as they are made in different sizes.   The wood must be well seasoned and dry or else the pins will soon become loose. This being so we must take care we don't split the corners off in doing our pins.

We use our long-cornered chisel just as though we were going to turn a pummel; that is the point of the chisel does the work.   The action of the tool is that it cuts through the fibres of the wood before it removes the wood as a shaving as in Fig. 8.   Please don't read on

makes very different tool action. In this principle is
important in many turning operations. The same way of
cutting is used in sawing a tenon shoulder and in long-
cornered chiselling; in both cases the tool is held so that
with it to form a wide curve, but otherwise similar to
shaving corners.

There is hardly any limit to the variety of the square and
curve treatment.

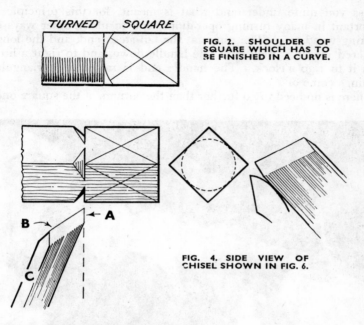

FIG. 2. SHOULDER OF
SQUARE WHICH HAS TO
BE FINISHED IN A CURVE.

FIG. 3. FIRST STAGE OF
REMOVING WASTE IN
CUTTING THE SHOULDER.

FIG. 4. SIDE VIEW OF
CHISEL SHOWN IN FIG. 6.

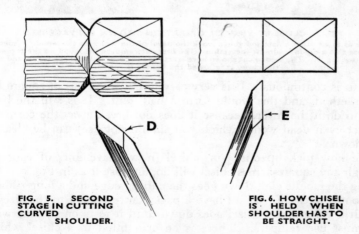

FIG. 5. SECOND
STAGE IN CUTTING
CURVED
SHOULDER.

FIG. 6. HOW CHISEL
IS HELD WHEN
SHOULDER HAS TO
BE STRAIGHT.

unless you quite understand what is meant, for this principle is important in many turning operations, and in many other ways of working wood too. The pin is at the tail-stock end, and the long-cornered chisel is held with the handle down, and to right a little with it to 1.30 o'clock. The handle end is raised and triangular shavings come off.

There is no need to go further than the corners of the square once

FIG. 7.   CLOSE-UP VIEW OF OPERATION SHOWN ON PAGE 108.
Here as in all other chisel and gouge work the bevel of the tool rubs the wood.   Unless it does this a dig-in is almost inevitable.   The first cut removes the wood on the turned side (see Fig. 3).   The second cut shown here starts at the outer point of the curve, and as the curve is followed the handle is raised.

the cut is continuous. It is very easy to cut wood out of square by this method, and this would form a bad joint. It is still the best way to do it, however, because it does not break away the corners; in fact even dead wood (which you should not use) can be cleanly cut down.

We now pick up our ½-in. chisel (if we have one, of course), though any square-across chisel will do, and use it as in Fig. 9. By lifting the handle end, down goes the cutting edge and a long ribbon of wood comes off. If we have a back centre turned to the size of the drill we use, the chisel goes down until it rests on it, otherwise we must use callipers. There is an arm fitted to a chisel which slides under the pin when it is to size, but this means that the chisel must be pushed forward, which is not cutting wood as it prefers to be cut.   If you study Fig. 10 (first position) you will note that the wood is rubbing *across* the cutting edge and so blunting it, and no nice long shaving is coming off.   In Fig. 9 you have easy control of the tool as its lower bevel is supported by rubbing on the work as well as on the rest; whereas in Fig. 10 the work is pulling the chisel

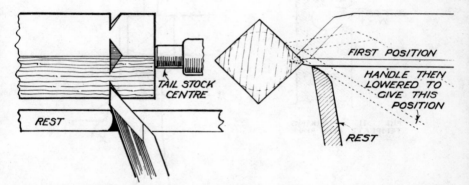

FIG. 8.   USING THE LONG-CORNERED CHISEL WHEN CUTTING THE SHOULDERS OF A PIN

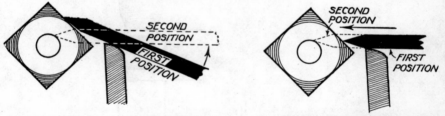

FIG. 9.   CUTTING THE PIN ITSELF USING THE ½ IN. SQUARE CHISEL.

FIG. 10.   LESS SATISFACTORY METHOD IN WHICH CHISEL SCRAPES.

down, and if the rest has to be well back from the work this can be a real difficulty.   It makes the tool chatter and, if it breaks the tool, you as well.

The best calliper to use is a slot cut in a stout piece of iron about ¼ in. thick as in Fig. 11.   You force it over the pin when nearly to size, and it bruises or nearly burns the pin to size (or shows that you have gone too far).   Just a touch with chisel over the rest of the pin clears it to size.   We have used this system for many years.   The iron bears on the rest, and is eased on to the pin as it might pull itself down and twist the pin off.   Remember that it is all done with the wood revolving.   It is well worth making for the pin sizes you use.

You may well think this a lot of fuss about a simple job.   Well pins are not so good as tenons for joints, but they are needed for some jobs, and in commercial work are often a necessity.

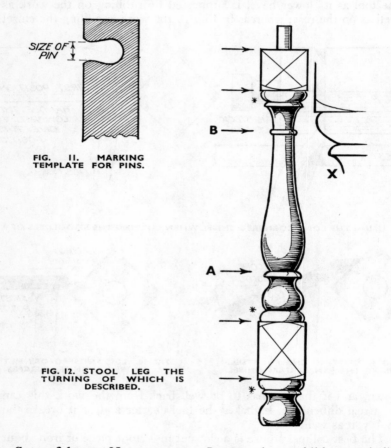

FIG. II. MARKING TEMPLATE FOR PINS.

FIG. 12. STOOL LEG THE TURNING OF WHICH IS DESCRIBED.

Sets of legs. Now years ago I counted my children and did four legs for each with four over, and made some delightful stools. I mention it here because they are a good example of the work I am talking about.   Sixteen legs had to be all alike as in Fig. 12.   The pin at the top had to go into an oblong ash seat 1 in. thick.   The four rails to fit in the bottom pummels had pins turned on them.   The first leg was turned to my liking and the wooden rest marked at positions shown by the arrows. This is how we do lots of work all alike in wood turning, and gradually the rest becomes marked by the tools.

Sometimes we use a carpenter's pencil and put a line on the wood, say, where the pummel is wanted. There is no need to mark all four sides of the wood, but it is best to use a square as it shows up much more clearly as the wood revolves if the line is square across the work. When a lot of work has to be marked we mark a pair of legs and lay a dozen or so between them. In some work it is best to put crosses on the pummels, as the pin might be turned into a foot in an unguarded moment.

Using the gouge. We have cut our leg down and rounded it, removing wood with the gouge to something like the general outline of the leg. Generally speaking, a gouge is the tool to remove wood and a chisel to pare it smooth with. Someone told me recently that the easy way I remove wood looks like murder. It is not clear just what was meant, but if you gently push someone over a cliff (please don't) he will do the rest himself. Well, if you hold the gouge to one side it will work itself along. In many turning jobs the tools do the job themselves; you just set the angle of cut. Blind men have a fine sense of touch and a St. Dunstan's man did a good job of turning recently, so I do urge you to try to find out the angles the tools work on and not to force or hold them too tightly. Just gently ease them about.

Our leg is roughed out and we cut little grooves with the corner of the long-cornered chisel at arrow (A, Fig. 12) and either side of arrow (B) which is a bead, and near the squares where the asterisks are. Some people put so many lines to guide them and use so many callipers that they cannot trust themselves to use their own eyes to guide them, so such beads, etc., are not marked. With our $\frac{1}{4}$-in. chisel we do the beads. I'm in favour of the shape as shown in Fig. 12 (X), as curves that cannot be done with a compass always seem better. These details give that individualistic appearance of your own work. The half beads are also done with the $\frac{1}{4}$-in. chisel and are that shape instead of being parallel so as not to reduce too much the hollow nearby.

Beads. If you are not good at turning beads just practise on a spare piece of wood, but don't develop the habit of using force or just scrape them to shape. If you persistently slip stop the lathe and peep underneath the tool and find out whether the tool is rubbing. The instructions are these: see that your chisel has an even bevel, not as you buy it. Hold its cutting edge on top of the wood so that it cannot cut, that is with the handle end low. Now turn the left-hand side of the bead. Move the handle slightly to the right and let the left-hand corner of the tool be in the middle of the bead, the cutting edge level to start with. Then, making the corner of tool do the work, raise the handle in a circular movement until the cutting edge is vertical. The lower side of bevel rubs all the way round, and the shape and size of bead is governed by the movement of the handle.

The other side of the bead is, of course, obvious but, as you become more skilful, less movement seems necessary, just as riding a bicycle which still must lean over in turning a corner. I could ride no hands, but cannot do turning no hands yet. On page 104 I describe the turning of larger beads with the gouge.

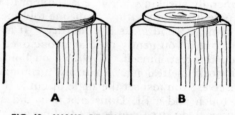

FIG. 13. WAYS OF FINISHING THE TOPS OF SQUARE LEGS.

The ½-in. chisel is best for the toe and larger curves, where exactly the same principle applies. The long curve is best done with the long-cornered chisel, and when near the little bead just push it forward so that the heel of the chisel cleans the corner out. The curve above the little bead is done with the gouge on its side at 9 o'clock, or our ¼-in. chisel could just clean the corner out. The small hollows such as in the foot are simple small gouge work. We gouge down from the large diameter to the bottom on one side and then on the other. The middle of the gouge (cutting edge, of course) does the work so that it is twisted in use from its side to lying level or at 12 o'clock in bottom of hollow. These gouges are ground a little to a point, but roughing-out gouges are square across.

Decorative cuts. Now if I told you pennies would cost you half-penny each you would think me crackers, yet that is the standard charge (my billheads had on them "Longest twisting experience in the trade"). Of course, there is a catch in it, and I am referring to the top of a leg which often has a turned patera on it. Craftsmen know that wood shrinks, and make allowance for it. Side rails of stools, etc., are not exempt from this law, and it is always towards the heart (I've gone the other way) except in a very few cases which need not concern us. So to save the leg standing proud at the corners we turn a little design on it, and then it does not matter. The simplest is a penny (A, Fig. 13), but a much nicer one is similar to draught-board checkers (B). This is done with a small gouge on its side, and ¼-in. chisel for the members. It is partly a scraping action as we are working on end grain.

The simplest stool of all to make is a milking stool, but do make it strong as so much relies on the fit of the legs in the seat. The seat can be turned with a slight hollow in the top and a groove round its edge. A nice scraper cut is ideal as little wood has to be removed. If the wood chatters owing to its hardness, or because the lathe is light, use a narrow cut. To avoid grooves when using narrow tools for face-turning set the rest parallel with the work and let the hand holding the tool slide along the rest. (Just a note to lathe manufacturers; we would like our rests parallel with no pieces sticking out as we slide our hands along them just as your slide rest goes along the lathe bed.) In fixing our stool legs we can drive them through the top and wedge them, cleaning all off flush with a scraper, or just make a good fit into a blind hole.

PARTING

The use of the parting tool can be most interesting. Amateurs find that they want to use it often, but the trade more often uses a circular saw which can part two thousand or so pieces an hour. It is entirely mechanical and far from interesting, though for joints a saw is ideal, since the uneven surface is excellent for glue.

Using the ¼-in. chisel. Let us take an actual example. First I tighten up the tail-stock to force the wood well on to the driving centre, and then ease it back a bit. The reason is that when the tool is nearly through the wood will collapse because of end pressure. Consequently I don't tighten the tail-stock more than is necessary to drive the work. It could be eased back just before final cut if you like. The ¼-in. chisel is not just pushed in, but rather the handle is raised. Fig. 14 shows how in this way the bevel of the tool rests on top of the work, holding it down as it is being cut. The tool will keep sharp much longer, too, since the wood is being cut as it prefers to be cut.

You will have noticed that a ¼-in. chisel has been mentioned, not a parting tool. That is because I want to show that a parallel tool is all right for parting with. If you have a proper parting tool which is relieved as in Fig. 15 by all means use it, but even so it is still good practice to do the following.   Just put your left hand around the work and ease it towards you, especially when nearly through.   This opens the slot, as in Fig. 16, and prevents the wood from binding on the sides of the tool.   Some use leather in the hand, but I don't recommend it unless you are thin-skinned.

Parting with the long-cornered chisel.   You will notice that

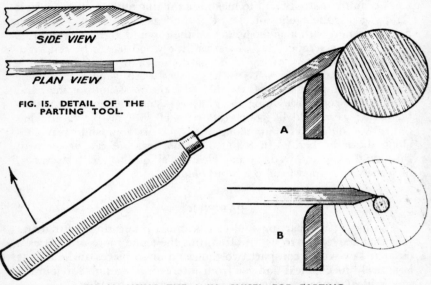

SIDE VIEW

PLAN VIEW

FIG. 15.   DETAIL OF THE PARTING TOOL.

A

B

FIG. 14.   USING THE ¼ IN. CHISEL FOR PARTING.
Note that the bevel rests upon the wood as at (A).   By raising the handle as at (B) the bevel still rests upon the wood.

the surface of the cut is rather sore as the fibres have been broken off, and not cut through.   There will also be the centre which breaks off as the wood collapses.   This may be an advantage in a joint to be glued, but if these things matter you can do a much cleaner job by using the long-cornered chisel.   It will use more wood to work in nicely and require more skill, but who is afraid to learn?   It is more difficult to describe too, but I'll try.   There are two quite distinctly different cuts involved, and when you have understood that it will help immensely to understand the principle involved.

The first cut makes shavings.   In the case of a square they are triangular in shape, but quite definitely shavings.   The handle end is lifted up as the cut is deepened (in the same manner as for the

¼-in. chisel), but is slightly to the left, too, as in Fig. 17. This is to avoid the corner of the chisel rubbing the work as in Fig. 19. The point end of the chisel is used and it is laid at an angle with the lower bevel rubbing the wood. If the shaving gets too wide to control the tool is tilted to a more vertical bevel so that the edge near the point does the work. The result of this cut is as in Fig. 17, but the surface is still sore as the fibres of wood are broken off.

Now we come to the second cut, and this does not remove a shaving so much as a fuzzy little ring of fibres. The point only of

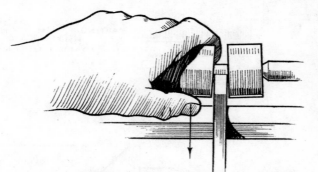

FIG. 16. PLAN VIEW OF PARTING WITH ¼ IN. CHISEL.
By pressing the work towards you (shown in exaggeration) any tendency for the chisel to bind is avoided.

the tool does the work. The bevel of the tool is lying against the finished end and as we raise the handle end of the tool up, the point goes down, just making a fine cut, and cutting cleanly from the part *we want left.* There seems to be a sort of satirical remark here, and I'll let you find out what it is, for good turning methods run very close to spoiling the job. Fig. 18 shows the position of the chisel as seen from above when making this second cut.

If you get the bevel wrong, or take too much, or have a slight burr on the point of the tool it will slip and spoil the job. Note I said "burr". Well, you can burn the point in grinding and so that the steel is soft and easily bends. Then again, as much cutting down is near the tail-stock centre, you may have just bumped into it, and caused a little burr. If you have watched me carefully at work, and I was anxious not to slip, my finger would just feel the point to see whether it was burred over. Sometimes tools fall down and it is invariably the point that catches it.

We have now one end nicely cut down and when you see the principle involved you can apply it to the other side of the cut.

Briefly the first cut removes wood in shavings, and the second cut pares a little off the part we want left. Figs. 20 and 21 show the two operations photographically.

There is still the very centre of the job to be parted, and a sudden break through might tear a little bit out. It is therefore advisable

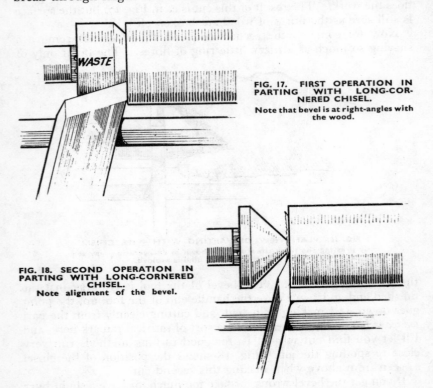

FIG. 17.   FIRST OPERATION IN PARTING   WITH   LONG-COR-NERED CHISEL.
Note that bevel is at right-angles with the wood.

FIG. 18. SECOND OPERATION IN PARTING WITH LONG-CORNERED CHISEL.
Note alignment of the bevel.

to make the final cut away from the finished surface and pare it off afterwards.

Specially ground parting tool. It may well be that this is too tedious and possibly you have a lot of discs to part cleanly off and don't want to use too much wood in the cut. An excellent idea is to groove your parting tool as in Fig. 22. The corners will cut through the fibres before the wood is removed just as in the case of a cross-cut saw. I've often told people to try to keep a sharp corner on their grinding wheels as this is just where you need it.

When I demonstrate I often turn little candlesticks and I turn a

candle down to about ⅛ in. diameter in the wood, and then boldly
part off the square at the base.   The secret here is a bold, steady cut,
for if you take too fine a shaving the wood just bends away, bounces
forward, and vibration sets up.   Don't be too bold, however.   You
can often damp out vibration or chatter in turning by increasing the
cut, but experience alone will teach just what you can do.   Besides
a bold cut I see that the parting tool is sharp on both corners and
that the bevel is rubbing on the work so as to avoid lifting the latter.

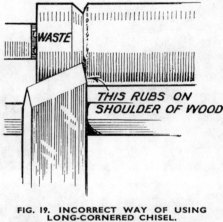

**FIG. 19. INCORRECT WAY OF USING
LONG-CORNERED CHISEL.**
The corner of the bevel rubs and cannot
give a square shoulder.

A miniature sundial has a thin top about $\frac{1}{16}$ in. thick and is left
the full size of the square.   For this it is essential to have a sharp
long-cornered chisel and to do exactly as described earlier, using the
two types of cutting, shavings, and ring of fibres.   The secret of not
knocking this thin square to pieces, however, is to not let the bevel
of the tool rub it hard and break it.   To the onlooker it looks just
the same as when I cut down, but the tool knows that I'm keeping
it away from exerting pressure on the work.

When you hold a lady's hand many subtle pressures may go on
quite unknown to others—my dear wife and I used to play guessing
tunes in this way as we went along.   You may ask what has this to
do with turning.   Well, my friends, the fact is that a gentle touch so
that you can feel the tool cutting is much better than force.   If the
tool digs in, it is being held at the wrong angle.   I do so stress this
because I've seen the joy many get in mastering the art, whilst

9—P.W.T.

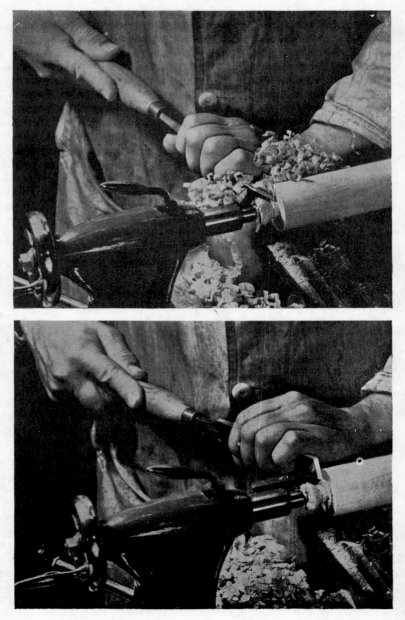

others simply will not hold the turning tools gently and feel them cutting, but rather force them about.

Please don't misunderstand me. I'm not advocating treating the wood gently, and taking off meagre shavings, for those who have seen me working know the reverse. "It's just murder to watch you and see how wood suffers," was a remark a large manufacturer of lathes said. But I feel the wood enjoys it, as my aim is to *cut the wood as it prefers to be cut*, and it must be much nicer to be murdered by someone enjoying it, than one who is afraid to do it, although I'm not speaking from experience—yet.

Turning a hollow. This frequently occurs in spindle work, and a common error is to use the gouge as in Fig. 23 with a scraping

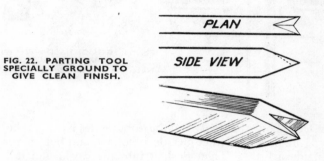

FIG. 22. PARTING TOOL SPECIALLY GROUND TO GIVE CLEAN FINISH.

action. It removes only dust and it leaves a ragged edge. In soft-wood the whole thing would be rough.

The proper way is to start with the handle well down, and the tool on its side with the handle over to the left when doing the right side of the hollow as at (A), Fig. 24. The handle end is raised, and the side of the gouge, with the bevel rubbing work, reduces the work. At the same time the gouge is twisted so that it is flat on its back when the centre of the hollow is reached (see A and B).

This twisting of the gouge makes it do the hollow itself as the bevel rubs against the work all the time. Of course you have to watch the curve of the hollow being generated, and that is where practice in twisting the tool about comes in. When I do this work I govern the thickness of shaving by how I lift the handle end, and continue the curve by how I twist the handle. The tool cannot dig

FIG. 20. (top left) **PARTING WITH LONG-CORNERED CHISEL.**
This is the first stage in which the bulk of the work is done. The chisel leans over at an angle.

FIG. 21. (bottom left) **SECOND STAGE IN PARTING.**
Here the bevel of the chisel is square to the work and only a thin shaving removed.

in because the bevel prevents it by rubbing the work. It keeps sharp longer because the whole of the cutting edge is used, not the point only; also because the wood does not move across the cutting edge but in line with it. Thus the shavings slide down the hollow.

A little experiment on a spare piece of wood may help you to

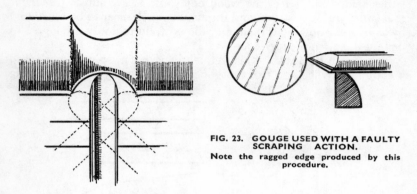

FIG. 23.   GOUGE USED WITH A FAULTY SCRAPING   ACTION.
Note the ragged edge produced by this procedure.

understand how the tools do the job themselves. Take a small gouge, $\frac{1}{4}$ in. or $\frac{3}{8}$ in. with a nice deep hollow, and hold it very lightly on its side a little. Then push it into the work, and it will itself slide to right or left, and the bevel will rub the work and do it. When I demonstrate this I hold the handle between two fingers, and place just one on top of the gouge near the rest to steady the tool. You can try twisting the handle too.

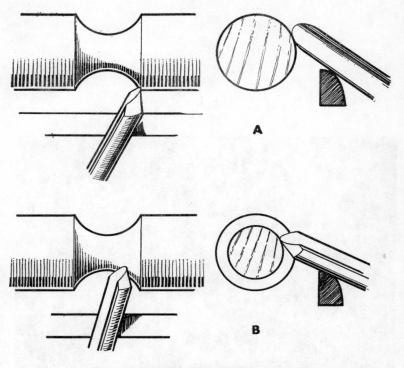

FIG. 24. CORRECT USE OF THE GOUGE.

The gouge is held on its side at the start and is twisted until by the time it has reached the centre of the hollow it is on its back. Note that the bevel is made to rub the work during the entire operation.

FIG. 25. METHOD OF STARTING THE CUT WHEN AN EXTRA DEEP HOLLOW IS REQUIRED.

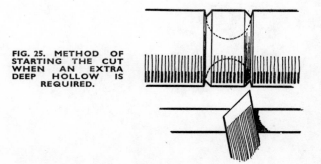

FIG. 26. TURNING END OF CYLINDER TO ROUNDED CURVE.

CHAPTER II : BORING HOLES

THE patron saint of wood-turning, St. Catherine of Alexandria, cannot help us much as history cannot prove that she ever lived (only that she died). We must share her with wheelwrights and mechanics for she is their patron saint too, but I feel sure you won't mind. I do not think she has been modernized so knows nothing about floor standards.

We are thinking about floor standards, and these do demand a high standard of workmanship and have their own problems too, such as boring long holes. Wood also is a problem (as apparently it was in 1417 A.D. when some wood-turners and clog-makers got into trouble for using wood good enough for arrows).

Boring long holes. Now the following is the quickest and best way of boring long holes that I know of. A judge, some prisoners, several ladies, and lots of boys have been successful at their first

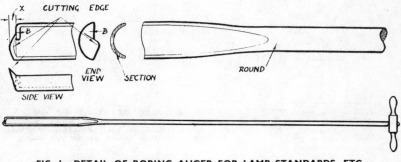

FIG. I. DETAIL OF BORING AUGER FOR LAMP STANDARDS, ETC.
Distance **X** gives thickness of cut. The rubbing portion B prevents the tool from digging in.

attempt. One boy at an exhibition does it blindfolded. The above is mentioned to give you confidence, and to knock the idea on the head that boring long holes is a difficult job. Incidentally, the boy at the exhibition put a bottle of pop under the bench. When he had bored the hole he went to it and held it up saying, "Now I know why I was blindfolded." You see the level had gone down quite a bit.

The boys put five holes down a 1¼-in. square 30 in. long, and three down a broom-stick, so it must be easy to bore one hole.

Auger and attachment. A special auger and attachment are needed, but if a school has a metal turning lathe it can be a joint operation. The auger is rather special, being made by a firm which

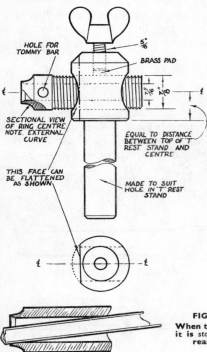

HOLE FOR
TOMMY BAR

⁵⁄₈

BRASS PAD

SECTIONAL VIEW
OF RING CENTRE.
NOTE. EXTERNAL
CURVE

THIS FACE CAN
BE FLATTENED
AS SHOWN

EQUAL TO DISTANCE
BETWEEN TOP OF 'T'
REST STAND AND
CENTRE

MADE TO SUIT
HOLE IN 'T' REST
STAND

FIG. 2. APPLIANCE FOR BORING.
The threaded tube is revolved so that it fits up to the wood and forms the back centre, being locked with the bolt at the top. The dowel at the bottom fits the T rest stand.

FIG. 3. AUGER AT START OF CUT.
When the auger is smaller than the hole in the tube it is *started* at an angle to save wobble. For this reason the tube should not be too long.

delights in awkward drills, etc., but its cost is only 9s. or so. Fig. 1 explains itself, and so long as the wood can revolve about 1,000 revolutions a minute all is well. The attachment, Fig. 2, is not intended to guide the auger, but rather to keep the wood up to the driving chuck. It has a hole for the auger to do its job. In some proprietary attachments, however, the hole in the tube is made to suit the size of boring auger being used. In this case it is essential that the tube is in perfect alignment with the work. For a simple job wood will do for the attachment with a tube fitted. Even a short piece of gas-pipe will do for the tube centre. The augers

sold sometimes have the parrot's nose end (see Fig. 9). These cut
cleaner holes than those square across, but can wander as the point
finds softer grain, so I advocate and always use the kind in Fig. 1.
Large holes 3 in. diameter and 6 ft. long are best done with the parrot
nose auger as this cuts a cleaner hole—short holes too if clean holes
are essential.   Large holes are needed for textile rollers, and if you
want a bit 10 in. in diameter with a cart-wheel on the end to rotate it
for boring wooden water pipes I know of one.

The boring operation.   The wood is revolving and we gently

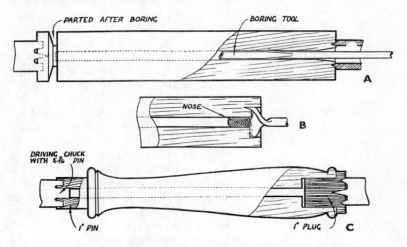

FIG. 4. STAGES IN BORING AND TURNING THE SHAFT.
A shows the boring operation. B gives the method of counter-boring with plug on nose
of bit. C is the I in. plug which fits in the back centre. Note also the special driving chuck.

push our auger slightly sideways into the hole of the attachment.
This is to prevent it from getting a wobble as it has no point.   So we
steady it as in Fig. 3, and for this reason don't have the hole in the
attachment too long.   The auger is held in one hand, and we don't
let it clog too much.   It is necessary to withdraw it from time to
time.   If you run the work too fast it will warm up, but don't go
too slow either—about 1,000 r.p.m. seems best.   At one school a
boy looked through while another blew all the dust into his eye; they
were so eager to see through it. (Note to instructors.   Don't tell
boys about blow-pipes with poisoned arrows, or pea-shooters.   It
holds up production.)

Counter-boring.   So the wood has a hole down it now, as at (A),
Fig. 4, and one end probably has to fit on to another piece, so we need

to counter-bore our $\frac{5}{16}$ in. or $\frac{7}{16}$ in. hole out to 1 in. diameter. This must be done carefully, and I suggest that you buy a 1 in. bit (other sizes are made) and fit a nose-piece on it as at Fig. 4 (B). Use either the chuck in your lathe, pushing the wood on to it, the bit revolving, or do it with hand brace. These bits cost about 2s. 10d., but one made for a machine costs 8s. 6d. or so, and is no better for the purpose. This type of counter-bore is suggested because the nose-piece will guide it to follow the hole already bored, and it has no part to catch into the sides of the hole after the cutting edge such as a long twist drill would have.

So our hole is true to size and parallel. It is an easy matter to turn a pin on the part to go into this hole, but don't hurry fitting it, as a sloppy fit is nothing to be proud of and will cause trouble.

To hold the work whilst this and the rest of the turning is done you can make a plug to fit the 1-in. hole and this run on the centre as at (C), Fig. 4. For the other end I once made a driving chuck with a $\frac{5}{16}$-in. pin on it to go into the hole as at (C), but never used it, so you can please yourself as it depends on your chuck diameter a bit, but undoubtedly a chuck with a pin to fit the hole is best.

Some of you may wish to screw the parts together. Well, thousands of gift standards were made that had a thread cut in them, but it powders away in use, and one man who did it is in a lunatic asylum, so be warned. If you must screw them, brass fittings are sold to fix on to the ends of the wood, but you have to recess the wood to take them. In any case screws don't hold well in end grain. When I fit parts together I try to match the grain. This, too, is against using these fittings.

Design. Whilst we are talking

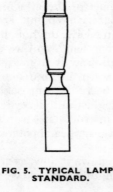

FIG. 5. TYPICAL LAMP
STANDARD.

about lamp standards we may as well briefly discuss the general work as well. The simpler the design the better it looks. You will find if you look around you that many beautiful things are quite plain except for some detail that holds your attention. The plain part is always nicely finished, however, showing up the grain of the material. A plain square tapered nicely and veneered with some beautiful wood is a joy to the maker, while a fussily turned column can be a worry. Turned details all the way up never look well. You can often copy the turning of the legs of a chair or table in the bottom half of a floor standard, the top half being a long gentle curve with an interesting detail to hold the lamp holder as in Fig. 5.

These long curves can be more trouble than a lot of hollows and beads, etc., as the line must be a nice gentle one. If you measure it as you go along all will be well. You will need a steady, and the best is that described on page 68. I can honestly say that I've never seen any other type used successfully in the furniture trade during the past fifty years. Some use lead weights on the wedge, some elastic, and some a screw to hold the wedge a little, but the principle is *right*. My living to-day is metal turning, and I am fully acquainted with the type of steady the engineer uses, but for wood it is not suitable. Floor standards are usually 5 ft. tall and so call for two 30 in. lengths of turning. A steady is a great help (though we can just manage without one).

I feel sorry for those who have to keep pushing the rest along the bed to turn another part. We always have a wooden rest long enough to do the whole job at once. If I say much more about lathe manufacturers, however, they won't like me, but it is obvious that a long, continuous flat curve needs a long rest so that the chisel can be taken along in an unbroken movement.

Base. Our base can be 12 in. or more diameter and it calls for a different treatment in design. The outline of the column is seen, but the reflections of light show the design of the base. There is another point. We often want the base to look thicker than it really is (this applies to bread-boards too). A few years back we used coffin boards to turn into bread-boards, and by Act of Parliament these were reduced from 1 in. to $\frac{3}{4}$ in. thick, but they looked nice as the shape made them look thicker. The section was quite simple (Fig. 6). It showed a broad surface at the outside and again the eye noted the inner bump, while the little sharp, hollow curve was not noticed unduly. Design is a subtle thing indeed, and often we can bring out more beauty by using a simple device. All true art uses skill, whether it be music, painting, or designing, to emphasize some point, and the result is much more interesting than plain mechanical curves.

So far we have the bottom part of the standard like the furniture it is to go with, and a nice heavy-looking base has been used. Straight lines always seem wrong mixed up with curves, yet much modern furniture is all straight lines.   If you do turn straight parts they always look better if slightly curved (? ?).

The joint in the column where it joins the base needs special treatment for it will show up the smallest difference in size, or any

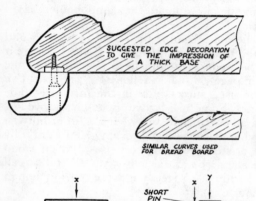

SUGGESTED EDGE DECORATION
TO GIVE THE IMPRESSION OF
A THICK BASE

SIMILAR CURVES USED
FOR BREAD BOARD

FIG. 6. SECTiON THROUGH BASE.

Also the special foot made with two centres.   This is provided with a short pin which gives exact positioning, and a counter-bored screw is driven through it to the base.

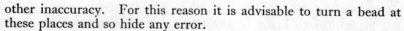

SHORT
PIN

Tw0 STAGES IN MAKING
THE FOOT
x, FIRST CENTRE
Y SECONED CENTRE

other inaccuracy.   For this reason it is advisable to turn a bead at these places and so hide any error.

At the base three toes are preferable as they always stand level. On the other hand four feet spread over a greater area and so help more in preventing the standard from falling over, so you can make your own choice.

To give our feet a wider area we can turn them on two centres, first as in Fig. 6 (left), then as at (right).   It is easy indeed to do and they peep out from under the base so to speak.   We found, however, that they were inclined to become loose as the pressure was not even.

We found that an ordinary screw was more satisfactory than a pin, so we used a short $\frac{3}{4}$ in. diameter pin with a screw running up its middle. This made a good strong fixing.

Larger holes. "A bung-hole without a barrel" won ten shillings in a competition to describe "nothing". It was sent in by one of my men, and his wife thought it very silly, but made a fuss of him when the money came. Well, in this chapter we are just thinking of holes. In wood-turning we soon find the need to bore a hole, although the local need for worm-holes in antique work has died out.

Let us now think of a really large hole such as that in a circular picture frame, or the front of a loudspeaker in a radio cabinet. In these the wood is mounted on the faceplate of the lathe. The chief troubles are springiness (unless the lathe is very solid), failing to cut cleanly, not to mention the liability to split right across.

Marking out. We will mark the size with pencil as the wood

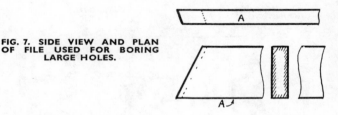

FIG. 7. SIDE VIEW AND PLAN OF FILE USED FOR BORING LARGE HOLES.

revolves. If you must use dividers just touch the side nearest to you with the point of the dividers on the rest, the other point against the far side of the circle you are scratching. Do not press against the revolving wood too hard or it certainly will catch in. You could set the dividers to half the size of the finished hole and put one point in the middle, which is easily seen as the work revolves. Personally, I much prefer to use a pencil and rule, as dividers do often catch in the revolving work.

Tool to use. An old file ground as Fig. 7 is needed, and please note that if the required holes are large only the end is bevelled, not either side. The tool is used practically level, just above centre height, and is simply pushed straight into the work. The bevel of the tool as seen from above keeps it against the finished hole, and as the side of the tool cannot cut it does not enlarge the hole, but keeps it parallel if the tool is square to the work. Should the tool be forced down it is also forced away from the wood into the scrap centre piece so the work is all right. That is why the sides of the tool have no (or very little) bevel.

The grain of the wood is cut cleanly through, and the bevel is still cutting the waste wood as it goes through so that the tool does not fall through suddenly owing to, say, a springy job.   If the tool were ground square across it would go through suddenly and might catch us out.   It certainly would not cut the fibres or grain so cleanly as a point would.

We could hold the work on a central screw in the waste centre piece or in other ways, according to the job.   It would probably be

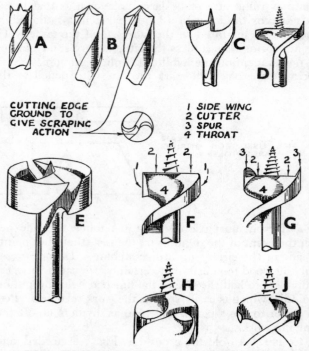

CUTTING EDGE
GROUND TO
GIVE SCRAPING
ACTION

1 SIDE WING
2 CUTTER
3 SPUR
4 THROAT

FIG. 8. TYPES OF DRILLS AND BITS USED IN BORING.
A. Specially ground drill for wood. B. Drills ground for brass. C. Simple centre bit. D. Special pattern centre bit. E. Forstner bit. F and G. Parts of bit: 1, side wing, 2, cutter, 3, spur, 4, throat. G. is the Jennings pattern bit. H. Solid nose bit. J. Gedge pattern bit.

a help to rest the elbow on the tail-stock to save the tool handle from moving about.   The same tool would help to bore out, say, cigarette boxes or powder boxes for "My Lady's" dressing-table.

You will find that deep holes have a way of becoming smaller the deeper you go, and it is necessary to see that the tool is presented square to the work to avoid it. The side of the tool could have a *little* bevel on it so that it just cuts the sides cleanly. It might well be a piece of oak you are working, and you find that the tool rakes out the fibres a bit when you are boring along the grain. Should you be troubled with long fibres coming out and spoiling the surface, make a final cut with the handle lowered slightly, and it will help. In the case of a cigarette box a disc could be turned to fit the hole and it could be finished off between centres as though it were a solid job.

Candlesticks. Early candlesticks did not have holes, but spikes. We do not use them to-day, however, so we will think of candlesticks with sockets. It is possible to buy candles from $\frac{3}{8}$ in. up to 2 in. diameter in over one hundred different sizes from stock. Much larger ones are also made—in fact, one special one is thirty-six feet tall—rather awkward in a house. It was lit in the Abbey where Queen Elizabeth was crowned and was an Easter candle to tell and remind us of the glorious message of Eastertide. The various sizes available are mentioned because it does seem nice to break away from the ordinary size; it is much more interesting and distinctive looking.

If any of you have tried to bore a candlestick after it has been turned you will have found that the drill just will not go where you want it to. You may also find that the thin neck is just not strong enough to take the strain of boring the hole, and something goes bust. The remedy is simple; bore the hole first, and let the centre run in it. If your centre is not long enough, at least start the drill. When we did that at the works it was a great improvement. It was one of those things that did not dawn on us for a few years, and perhaps it has not on others. We used a twist drill sharpened as at (A), Fig. 8. The drill revolved in the lathe and the work was pushed by the tail-stock centre, being held from rotating by the hand.

You will find that drills, augers, twist bits, etc., which are parallel, or nearly so, have a habit of getting out of control if the work is allowed to move sideways at the end. The sides of the drill catch the sides of the hole and wrench it out of your hand. So, although you might be strong enough to push the wood, it is advisable to use the tail-stock centre to steady the end. You must keep the wood against the centre as you bring it back, too, or at least pull it back carefully. In these matters I do advise you to see just what happens, as some drills are more prone to this than others, and by their faults ye shall know them.

Kinds of drills. I've two catalogues of about 120 pages with different drills on each page, so you see there is a large range to choose from.   I go to a lot of trouble to find out the best, though, of course, I have not come across every sort in my work.   (Not many of you want a 3-in. bit 6 ft. long, or one costing £25.)

A drill will bore fairly truly across the grain—that is like boring towards centre of tree.   We come to a hard layer of grain, then a soft layer, and the drill keeps fairly true.   We can also drill truly with the grain.   So now picture, say, a cross with a central ball across which we wish to drill a hole.   If we drill parallel with the grain or across it all will be well.   Just to see clearly what a drill does, you could get a round piece of wood like a broomstick and drill holes across it.   You will see how most drills wander.

In, say, a disc to hold three lights we must drill at an angle to the grain, of course, and I have found that the Jennings pattern bit is good, the dowel type (which is short) being the best.   First, however, we bored with a $\frac{1}{8}$-in. twist drill, and the centre of the bit followed that hole.   Of course, we could have fixed the job into a drilling machine, and had a stiff twist drill which would go where it was forced to, but this is not the way for amateurs.

Sharpening bits.   I think it would be helpful here to quote from the makers, Messrs. Ridgway (who only sell to shops) the instructions on sharpening (I've their permission to quote them).

"Generally speaking, bits are sharpened more often than necessary, and the life of many is considerably shortened by incorrect filing.   Carefully examine a bit before sharpening, and when filing endeavour to keep to the original shape.   Keep the balance of the nose of a bit.   Each side should do the same amount of work and to ensure this always file both sides equally.   Use a smooth file, and file lightly with the object of removing only as little metal as is necessary.

"*Sharpening the side wings*.   Rest the bit on the bench with the screw lead down.   Work with the file passing through the throat of the bit.   Never file the side wings on the outside, or the clearance will be spoilt.

"*Sharpening the cutters*.   Hold the bit in the same way as you would to sharpen the side wings, and file the cutting edges on the underside only, i.e. with the file working through the throat of the bit.   It is essential that the cutters should be at the same level so that they cut chips of equal thickness.

"*Sharpening the spurs*.   Hold the bit, nose uppermost, with its twist firmly against the edge of the bench.   File the inside of the spur.   Never file the outside, as this reduces the clearance, and causes binding and clogging when boring.   Never attempt to sharpen a bit by grinding."

Well, the above is the maker's advice, and I agree very much with it.

Clean holes. I think a few thoughts on boring clean holes may help here, and let us start with the Jennings type. The spurs cut through the fibres before the cutters remove the wood, and this is an ideal state of affairs. The screw is either in a small hole already bored, or it is made into a brad point (like a pyramid) so that it does not pull in. These last remarks are for the bit when used in the lathe; we want the screw if we are using the bit in a hand-brace.

Now there is another way of cutting a clean hole, and that is using a curved nose. Fig. 9 shows a spoon bit of the type at (K). It was widely used in the chair trade at one time. The bench was low, about 12 in. from the floor, and three wooden pins stood up,

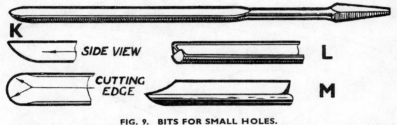

FIG. 9. BITS FOR SMALL HOLES.
K. Spoon bit with enlarged views below at left. L. Special auger for deep holes. M. Parrot nose bit.

as in Fig. 10. A wedge held the legs to be bored. Since a part of a spoon bit rubs, it was always dipped into a box of grease before each hole was bored. The bit is rather a job to start as it has no point, and it is turned both ways with quite a pressure on the hand-brace. The workman wore a curved piece of wood on his chest so as to spread the strain a bit. It did bore a clean hole because of its curved nose.

Parrot-nosed bits (M), Fig. 9, Gedge's pattern (J), Fig. 8, solid nose with holes in it (H), Fig. 8, and others have a similar principle, and if you think you will see why the sides of the hole are nice and smooth. This Gedge's or solid-nose pattern bit is good to bore a hole at an angle; in fact, when the screw is in a little way you can carefully move the bit over, as there is no spur as in a Jennings type to catch into the work.

Principle of the drill. It may be as well to consider why drills, etc. are made as they are, as if you sharpen them wrongly you will have trouble. You will notice there is a part of the drill rubbing the work and preventing it from pulling in. A twist drill is ground at its nose at about the angle of its feed and it is a mistake to bevel it too much. The square-nosed bit I advocate for boring long holes —three down a broomstick blindfolded—has a part of the auger to rub on the opposite side of the cutter (L), Fig. 9. A Jennings (G), Fig. 8 and similar bits have the cutter at an angle so that it is prevented from pulling in. The makers say, don't alter it, so keep your files off it and try to see just which part of the drill prevents this pulling-in effect, or you may not enjoy boring holes.

Twist drills for boring wood are ground as at (A), Fig. 8, using the corner of the wheel. In the furniture trade they have a $\frac{3}{8}$ in.

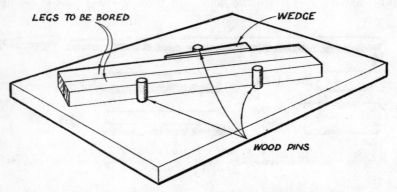

LEGS TO BE BORED   WEDGE

WOOD PINS

FIG. 10. HOW CHAIR PARTS ARE HELD WHEN BORING.

diameter thread on them to screw into the drilling machine. This is because a bunch of drills for boring holes for dowels is used together and there is no room for a chuck. When the drills become too short they are discarded. Some are left-handed to suit the machine, and so you have a left-handed drill.

Twist drills are meant for metal, of course. For iron they are all right as sold, but if you find it hard work, just a little touch on the wheel as at (B), Fig. 8, does help immensely. I always try to keep a corner on my grinding wheel for this purpose. Now brass ought to have a straight twist drill—no, I mean a straight-fluted drill with no twist. Personally, however, I find a twist drill better, but altered as at (B), Fig. 8. It is only a trifle, not enough to get to the relieved part, or it will be hard going. If you don't do it the drill pulls through and becomes seized. An oilstone could alter the drill, and is well worth doing if you drill brass.

Some bits must involve complicated methods of manufacture. I am thinking of a Forstner bit (E), Fig. 8, which will bore cleanly a flat-bottomed hole. It will also bore at any angle, and even bore half a hole. You could use it on your table and cut hollows out on the edge. Overlapping holes, too, can be bored and the direction of the grain does not affect it. It is an expensive bit, however, as it is so awkward to make. They are made up to 2 in. diameter.

I've hardly touched on drills, but do hope those I've mentioned may help you to understand those you come across. Special jobs need special drills; some are for wet wood and generally cut one side only; some are for heavy work where clean cutting is not necessary. If you use one having a screw point in the lathe or drilling machine do either bore a small hole first so that screw does not pull in, or alter it to a brad point. Of course, if your lathe goes slowly, all is well, but few do. Many of you probably only want to bore a few holes, and hand-drills are much cheaper than machine bits, so that may help save £ s. d. I used them for years. I sawed off the square that goes into the brace and used them in my drilling machine.

The makers are trying to popularize a short drill, like a Jennings at the end, but having only half a turn of twist (D), (Fig. 8). It seems a good idea as a long twist part is not always wanted. They are to take the place of the carpenter's centre bit (C), Fig. 8, which needs pushing. During the war I bored holes for those walkie-talkie sets, and got some out of truth. They were about 8 ft. long, and I enquired what error I was allowed and was told 3/1,000 in. I asked the man how he tested them and he replied that he had good eyesight. Well! I do believe in accuracy in holes, but to put 8 holes in 8 ft. accurately to that error is fairly good going (if we did?). Well, I hope you have not been bored, and will be able to bung holes in wood.

CHAPTER 12 : SOME GENERAL HINTS

HOW TO FEEL COMFORTABLE

IT is difficult to do good work if you do not feel comfortable, and you certainly will not enjoy your hobby if you are working in a strained position. Here I hope to show you how you can enjoy wood turning more comfortably.

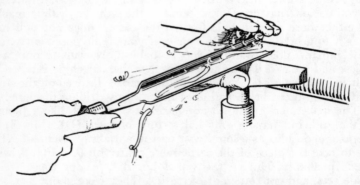

FIG. I.   PREVENTING CHIPS FROM FLYING INTO THE FACE.
By cupping the fingers over the tool the chips can be deflected.

Dust.   Let us first consider the eyes.   The chief worry from our point of view is dust, or rather chips of wood.   Professional turners do not wear protective glasses; they cup their hands over the flying chips or direct them elsewhere than into their face as in Fig. 1.   In my experience people find it a job to do this, possibly because they want to see the tool cutting whereas the professional turner looks on the outline of the job more and feels the tool doing its job.

If you do not wear glasses, perhaps a pair of goggles will help to give you confidence against the chips entering your eyes (Fig. 2). There is no need for special ones as I have never heard of chips breaking the glasses.

Now, all the people I know have the habit of breathing and so you can take in dust.   The fact is, however, that there ought to be little dust if you cut the wood cleanly.   When glasspapering you cannot help it, except by seeing where it goes and dodging it.   So far as I

140

know it is nothing much to worry about—not like the dreaded disease miners and masons can get. I suppose it is not exactly good for you (certain fancy woods can give you a cold in de nose) but, my friends, do not worry about it. Just keep on breathing. Personally I have grown fat on it.

Satin wood and a few other species can cause little pimples on the skin of some people, but little of the wood is about now. Twenty per cent, used to be added to wages when it was worked, but few people were affected by it. Dust can cause dermatitis of the skin to some people, but it is comparatively rare and is similar to that which bakers get, and is hardly worth even thinking about.

Dress. Your neck may well catch the shavings, and your bedroom floor will tell the tale when you undress (not to mention feeling the chips working themselves down or getting stuck half way down). The fourteen turners we had always had a carpenter's apron on and by a knot made it tight under the chin. It is better than a smock dust coat. For myself I wore a scarf and some declared it was never tight enough. Anyhow, my lady of the house will welcome less chips about, and on this score remember that the turn-ups of trousers can bring home the chips. There are some lady turners and they solve the problem quite happily.

FIG. 2. SOME MAY PREFER TO USE GOGGLES.

Height. When you stand upright and put your hand to your shoulder, the elbow is just a happy height for the centre line of the lathe (see page 9). Most likely yours is too low (many are) and you have to bend over, getting the dust in your face and developing backache too. The remedy seems obvious, and you may wonder why manufacturers make their lathes so low. The answer one gave me was that so many of their lathes go to schools. It seems a fair answer, but we hardly go on using our children's push-bikes so let us have a lathe to suit our height and avoid backache —let gardening provide that.

Hands. Somewhere I have read that one should not let the left hand know what the right one is doing, but it could hardly have been a talk about turning. The two hands work in harmony. The following is written chiefly for right-handed people and I hope that left-handed people will see what I am getting at and apply the idea to themselves. For my part I am ambidextrous (besides being other things, as I am told). The actual movement the tools require for the various operations is dealt with elsewhere, and these remarks concern the way the hands can do it. Some teachers lay down hard-

and-fast rules, but I think the fact is that we all work out ways which suit us.

Broadly speaking it does not matter a lot. The way most professional turners work is that the right hand holds the end of the handle in an easy way so that he can twist it on its axis or raise and lower it. We are thinking now of spindle work such as a chair leg. The left hand has the thumb under the tool, and four fingers above in an arch to trap the shavings from flying into the face as in Fig. 3. There is a meaty part of the hand opposite the thumb and this rubs comfortably along a wooden rest, which is (or should be) parallel.

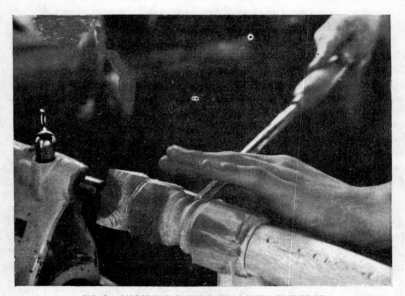

FIG. 3. AVOIDING CHIPS FLYING INTO THE FACE.
Some people find it distressing to have a stream of chips flying into the face. Arching the fingers over the tool prevents this.

Manufacturers invariably sell metal rests and often make them a fancy shape, whereas we just want a simple parallel one. Wood is nicer to feel in any case. Some metal rests are the right shape although they taper at the ends. If your hand holding the tool slides along parallel with the work, all is well. Should your rest be wrong perhaps a file will help matters—but why should they be made wrong?

Tapered work. We have been thinking so far of the hand

moving along the rest as, say, for a rolling-pin. Let us now consider taper or shaped work. Here the tool must go forward, for we always work from the larger diameter to the smaller. So you can picture the meaty part of the left hand against the rest with the tool held between thumb and fingers and eased towards the work without loosing the steadying anchor on the rest. What I'm trying to say is that we don't advance the tool by first having the hand away from the rest so losing the steadying effect. Rather we manipulate the hand without shifting it from the rest.

Some chisels, especially wide ones, have to be kept at a certain

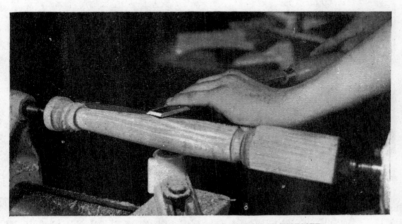

FIG. 4. HOW LONG TAPERED WORK IS TURNED.
Keep the left hand on the rest and ease the tool forward, the grip being maintained without shifting the position of the hand on the rest.

angle. They don't lie flat on the rest. The thumb underneath with the fingers on top and perhaps curled around the chisel will help nicely here. Fig. 4 shows the method well. The weight of the hand has a good effect in holding the tool down, sometimes damping out vibrations. When we turn long, slender work our right-hand fingers can curl round the work with the thumb only on the chisel to hold it down as in Fig. 5. This is a nice way of steadying the work and is quite safe. It is often a help against ribbing, and you don't really wear through to the bone. You stand with the left side of the body nearer to the lathe, just sideways a little.

Face plate work. In face-turning work, say the inside of a bowl, the flat scraping tools lie flat on the rest with the cutting edge pointing slightly downwards. The right hand holds the end of the

tool. The grain of the wood does sometimes tend to make the tool
wobble up and down, but it can easily be checked by resting the
elbow on the tail-stock, which is not in use. We wish to push this
tool evenly into the work and we can anchor the palm of the hand
on the end of the rest. By closing the hand we can bring the tool
along the rest, the thumb not being used. One word of warning.
You can be so occupied in thought about the tool that the hand rubs
the bowl and this is not nice.

Some find the shavings sting them as they fly off and gloves might

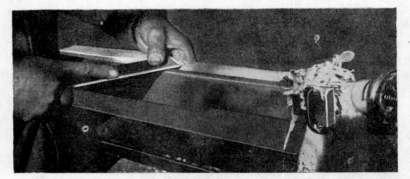

FIG. 5. CHISELLING A LONG CYLINDER, FINGERS AROUND WORK.
This is a specially useful method for long slender work. It is a great help in avoiding
ribbing.

help here, but do take care that they don't get caught in revolving
parts. A coat sleeve caught on a shaft coupling at my works caused
a man to lose an arm. Admittedly that was using big power but I
say again be careful if you use gloves. Should you find that you
get on better by gripping the tool with the fingers underneath and
the thumb on top, well it's a free country, but you cannot check
the shavings as they fly off—but then you may not want to. For
small intricate work this is quite a good way to control the tool,
and you can still hold the fingers against the rest to govern the feed.

Elsewhere I've written, don't hold the tools tightly. There is no
need to make your muscles tense in wood turning and so tire yourself.
My aim in developing a light touch is that the tools convey to you
how they are getting on. You feel it and know when all is well or
that a chatter has been set up requiring an alteration of tool angle
somewhere. The tools do all the work and you have only to just
move them about (although there does seem to be an art in it somewhere). If you have to use brute force to move the tools about your
methods are wrong.

Lighting. Bad lighting can worry you. In a new factory we went modern and had tubular lights fitted, but the men asked for the old system back again, just electric bulbs in shades to prevent the light from falling on their eyes. A window in front of you is ideal and no skylight. Perhaps when you have been driving your

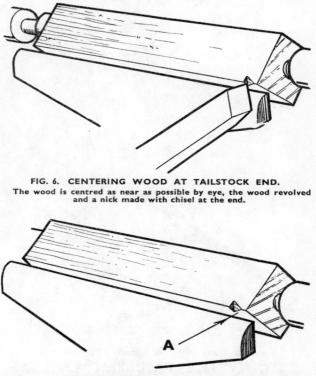

FIG. 6. CENTERING WOOD AT TAILSTOCK END.
The wood is centred as near as possible by eye, the wood revolved and a nick made with chisel at the end.

FIG. 7. HOW NICK REVEALS WHETHER WOOD IS CENTRED.
If only one corner is nicked as at (A), or if one corner is nicked more than the others, give the wood a knock with the chisel in the direction shown by the arrow.

car at night-time you have noticed how the headlights have shown up the unevenness of the road. This is just where tubular lights fail, for we wish to see the undulations of the shapes and the older type of light shows this better.

Centering. It is often recommended that you mark the ends of the wood to find the centre of the square but you will find it seldom runs true this way as the point wanders to a soft part of the grain. I do not recommend this way except for squares of over 3 in. diameter. The trade way is to put the wood between centres as true as you can guess it, with the back centre only slightly screwed up, and just nick the corner as it revolves as in Fig. 6. We then hold the wood still, and give this corner a biff with the chisel (for we certainly have no time to pick up anything else) as in Fig. 7 and

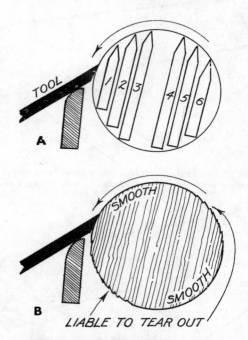

FIG. 8. LIABILITY OF GRAIN TO SPLIT.
(A) shows imaginary pencils on a face plate, tool being used at the edge. Pencils 5 and 6 are liable to break away. The actual wood is shown at (B) and the tendency of the corresponding parts to split is shown.

tighten the back centre. We never stop the lathe, but probably it would be better if you do. Certainly this method soon finds fault with a bad pair of centres, but then why have them wrong?

If your centre bends in use tell the makers about it. I've been instrumental in improving some, but why some lathes are fitted with such poor centres beats me. I've purposely bent some. You must excuse my remarking about centres, but I am sure that many have no idea how a nice happy pair of centres give joy in their use, and save excessive pressure on the bearings too.

Face plate work.   As many of my followers are not in the wood line I am putting in this next bit to help them understand wood better.   I've shown in Fig. 8 a disc of wood on a face plate and pictured it at (A) as a lot of pencils, as I feel some may understand this better.   Only the pointed ends are referred to in the text. One of my slogans is *"cutting wood as it prefers to be cut,"* and pencil No. 1 is ideally placed. whereas No. 6 is like trying to sharpen a pencil from the point inwards.   It is clear, then, that we cannot apply our slogan in this case, so we must see what we can do about it.

The tool is shown on the edge of the disc in Fig. 8 (B), but in Fig. 9 the tool is at the face of the disc.   It is something like laying our pencils on the table and forcing a chisel down across the grain.   This is not such a nice way to cut wood, but splits won't occur, such as in pencil No. 6 in Fig. 8.   Thus it is an improvement to work across the disc rather than on the edge.

Now Fig. 9 shows a square piece which we wish to turn round (when in business we often had similar jobs as it saved sawing). The end view shows the tool, and please note we are aiming at just turning a round disc, which could be a toy wheel, egg stand, bread board, or base of table lamp when finished.   The tool shown is a flat scraper tool, and part (A) is doing all the work, and this is on the waste wood.   The point of the tool is just cutting across the fibres of grain (which is really our trouble) and these fibres are held by the disc proper at one side, and by the waste piece of wood at the other.

If we were to work on the edge of the wood the tool could easily split the grain off, and it could be dangerous.   By working from the face, however, we are not in line and when the waste flies off it only goes through the window.   If your finished disc must have a good edge, either reverse the wood on the face plate, or go slowly, as it could break away a bit on going through.

From the above you will see that it is often desirable to work from the face rather than the edge in face-turning, and also to have the tool flat.   In this way the grain of the wood is held from both sides, and so is cut across without splitting.   A properly sharpened cross-cut saw uses the same principle.   The point of each tooth cuts cleanly, and the wood is removed as sawdust by a bevel.

Unseasoned elm.   Now recently it was my birthday, and it was so successful that I think I'll have another one soon, as so many boxes of sweets came.   Well, some humbugs in a tin seem hygroscopic; that is, they like moisture (one of my men liked moisture too, but not water); and some wood, notably elm, is the same.   We have

to use heat to dry it out, though steam is used in the trade.   On
its own it just remains wet and goes rotten with fungus.   It can be
as much as half water by weight, yet elm, by its short grain and the
fact that it does not split easily, is a good face-turning wood.   Wood

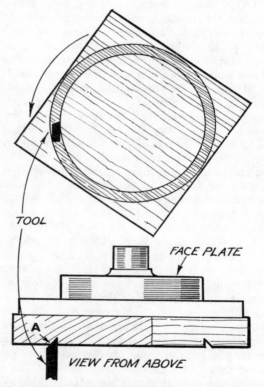

TOOL

FACE PLATE

A

VIEW FROM ABOVE

FIG. 9. TOOL USED FROM FACE RATHER THAN EDGE.
The tool is used with a scraping action, the cut at (A) being on the
waste wood.

is best shaped to nearly the finished size, then seasoned and finished
off.   This, in the case of the elm, prevents fungus from starting,
avoids surface splits, and allows for all sorts of warping and internal
stresses.   In its fresh state we can turn it easily.   A 10-in. disc
can shrink $\frac{5}{8}$ in. or so, and lose half its weight in drying.   When
in business and roughing out elm bowls the sap was flung out by
centrifugal force, and ran down the walls.

I think we can say with such a variety of wood to choose from and with such a lot of troubles it is heir to, wood can be extremely interesting.   Each wood seems to have good and bad points, but so much wood in England has in the past been like Topsy in Uncle Tom's Cabin; it just growed.   No doubt we do get unsuitable wood. English oak will easily split except where grown on boggy soil, whereas Austrian and Polish oak is ideal for carving or for turning bowls, and is very mellow.   American oak is different again.

Ring shakes.   In this one year's ring does not join on to the previous year's, and turned work can split lengthwise down that year in a way that will quite surprise you.   Altogether, wood is a complex material, prone to all sorts of troubles, and our designs and work must allow for it.   Some woods become quite brittle and short in the grain with age (mahogany does), and in this state can be weak for such purposes as legs, etc.   Oak seems to improve with age, both in colour and working, but dead wood is of no use to turners, and some drying methods can cause this.

Some of my friends find that about six weeks in a warm airing cupboard is right for elm, but you can observe this for yourself better than I can advise, as conditions vary so.

POLISHING IN THE LATHE

(continued from page 163)

rather hard and not too wide an area, moving it slowly from one part of the bowl to the other as the lathe revolves, a sort of burnishing action of *once only*.   If you start too soon, you just wipe it off; if too late, you have to bear too hard on to the work and burnt ribs of stuff result, but when you have found the knack it is extremely easy to get a quick shine.   We sometimes used a pullover both on cellulose and shellac polish, and the action is that it softens the surface and by gentle holding of the rag smooths the surface better.   The trouble when using a lathe for polishing is that you want eight or more in a row so that the work has time to harden a bit.

One last thought.   A boy finished off with water may be far better to look at than someone done in a special beauty creation. So first a good surface, then a thin clear polish that does not hide the beauty.

In rather a famous church I noticed that the font cover, which was very elaborate, was covered with thick varnish.   It was to strengthen it I was told.   Personally I believe I've got to that stage when varnish is needed; I wish I was a boy.

CHAPTER 13 : DECORATIVE TURNERY

THIS is the name often given to turned items which are inlaid or built in various ways. The work is done almost entirely in the lathe, though for some operations the tool revolves and the work is pushed up to it. Some extremely attractive work can be made in this way, an example being given in Fig. 1. The main part of the bowl is of oak relieved with sycamore, with inlays of cocus and tulip

FIG. 1. ATTRACTIVE OAK BOWL AND LID WITH HARDWOOD INLAYS.
The entire work including the inlays can be done on the lathe.

wood. The whole process is carried out on the lathe. It makes a delightful bowl, extremely rich in appearance, and is excellent practice in careful, accurate turning.

As a good deal of work is put into the bowl it is well worth while to make sure that the timber is of first quality, sound, nicely figured, and seasoned. It would be annoying later to have trouble due to

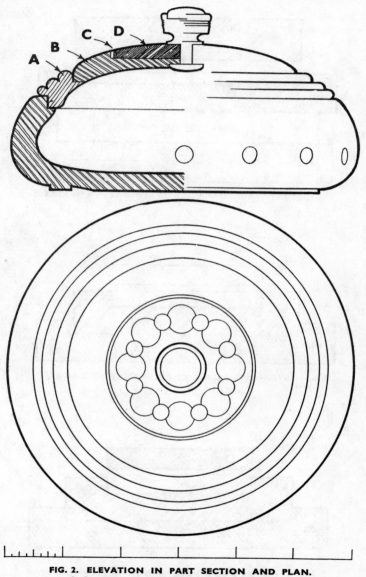

FIG. 2. ELEVATION IN PART SECTION AND PLAN.
A. Sycamore.   B. Oak.   C. Sycamore.   D. Cocus.

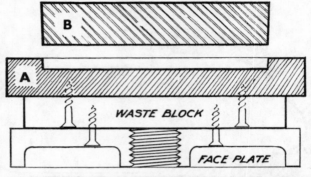

FIG. 3. FIRST STAGE, OAK PIECE (B) BEING LET INTO RECESS
TURNED IN SYCAMORE (A).

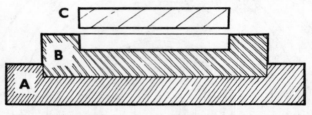

FIG. 4. SYCAMORE INLAY (C) RECESSED INTO OAK (B).

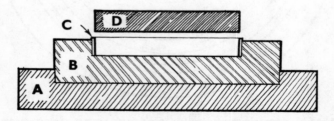

FIG. 5. COCUS DISC (D) RECESSED INTO SYCAMORE (C).

movement.   Since the majority of the work is put into the lid it is advisable to make this first and turn the bowl to it.

Lid.   From Fig. 2 it will be seen that the lid consists of a ring of sycamore (A) beaded in section with a main oak portion (B) let into it.   Within this again is a ring of sycamore (C) encircling a cocus portion (D), this being inlaid with inlays of sycamore and tulip.

Begin by turning the oak piece (B).   Fix a waste piece of hardwood to the face plate with screws, turn its face true, and glue the oak to it with a piece of newspaper interposed.   Turn the oak to the finished size with the edges *very* slightly tapered towards the side to be glued.   Lever away from the waste and clean off the paper.

Now prepare the sycamore (A), cutting out a disc of $\frac{3}{4}$-in. stuff to finish $5\frac{1}{4}$ in. diameter.   Fix it to a piece of waste hardwood with screws driven through the latter as in Fig. 3.   Put the screws well

FIG.   6.   SPECIAL
SCRAPING TOOL
FOR   TURNING
SMALL   BEADS.

in from the edge in positions where they will be removed when the inside is turned later.   Fix the waste to the face plate with screws. Once again the waste piece must be trued up beforehand by turning it before fixing the sycamore.   Turn the latter slightly full in size and form a recess in it as at (A), Fig. 3 to receive the oak (B).   The edges of the recess should be at a slight angle to align with those of the oak, but the latter must bed right down.   The simplest way is to turn the recess slightly small and gradually enlarge it to take the oak, constantly trying the latter in position for size.   Leave the sycamore in position on the face plate.

Glue in the oak, and when dry turn a recess to receive the sycamore (C) as in Fig. 4.   Once again glue in and, when set, turn a further recess to receive the cocus disc (D), Fig. 5.   The sycamore ring can be a bare $\frac{1}{16}$ in. wide.   Both (C) and (D) are turned on the screw chuck.   Glue in (D), and the whole is then ready for turning to the finished shape.   Turn to the main curve first, and nick in where the sycamore separates from the oak.   It is advisable to use scraping tools throughout.   A special tool can be ground to form the beads as in Fig. 6.

All the inlaid circles in Fig. 2 are centred on a common circle.

To ensure their being correct turn a scratch (no more) in the correct position.   The large inlays are put in first, and their centres are best marked by stepping around the scratched ring with dividers.   It is advisable to prick the final marks deeply.   Place a centre bit with round shank in the lathe, using the drill chuck or self-centering chuck. Hold the work by hand so that its surface is as near as possible square with the bit.   It is a help to bring up the back centre to steady and position the work.   Bore each hole about ⅛ in. deep.

The inlays can be turned in a row between centres as in Fig. 7. Note that the grain runs crosswise.   Separate them and glue them into their holes so that they stand proud.   When dry turn down level and bore the holes for the smaller inlays.   Glue in as before, and turn finally to the finished shape.   Also bore the centre hole for the handle.   Note that in the entire process the work has not been

**FIG. 7.   TURNING   IN-
LAY.
Note direction of grain.**

removed from the face plate.   Parts (C) and (D) can be turned on the screw chuck, or held in any other convenient way.

To turn the inside to shape fix a waste piece to the face plate, and turn a recess in it to take the lid.   The curve need not align closely, but there should be an accurate fit at the edge.   Fix with a bolt passed through the centre hole.   Turn down to shape, leaving a "pillar" at the middle.   Finally turn in a recess to receive the hiding button.   When the bolt is removed the pillar can be snapped off, levelled, and the button glued in.

Bowl.   This calls for no special instructions.   The best way is to fix the wood with the top against the face plate and turn the base with its rim and recess for the leather facing.   It is removed, and a waste block screwed to the face plate.   A recess is turned in this to take the rim (accurate fit), and the bowl glued in with waste paper interposed so that it can be levered away later.   This enables the sides and the inside to be turned.   The dots are bored and inlaid similarly to those of the lid.

Built-up bowl.   Another popular form of decorative bowl in which a number of small pieces of wood are glued together is that shown in Fig. 8.   The segments are assembled in layers and these glued together.   An almost unlimited variety of designs is possible.

The way in which the parts are assembled is the chief factor in the resulting pattern. That shown in Fig. 8 is one of the simplest. There are three rings, each of twelve pieces mitred together. In the assembling of the rings the joints are staggered, so that the pieces lie above each other brick fashion. One advantage of the method is that it enables oddments of wood to be used up.

In the bowl in Fig. 8 only two different kinds of wood are used.

FIG. 8. BUILT-UP BOWL SHOWING THE "BRICKS"
This is a simple pattern with three layers, each of twelve "bricks." More elaborate
designs could be worked out on the same principle.

Any number could be employed, each ring having its own particular woods, or they could be distributed generally. One important point is to avoid using woods of widely varying hardness, as this may cause difficulty in the turning owing to the tool pressing more into the soft woods than the hard ones. Apart from this the choice is unlimited. It is always an advantage to have an even number of pieces to each ring for a reason that will appear later.

Setting out. To enable the sizes and angles to be ascertained a full-size drawing such as that in Fig. 9 is needed. In this particular instance there are twelve pieces to each ring, but this could be increased for a larger bowl. The section will reveal the width required for the blocks to enable the shape to be worked. Be

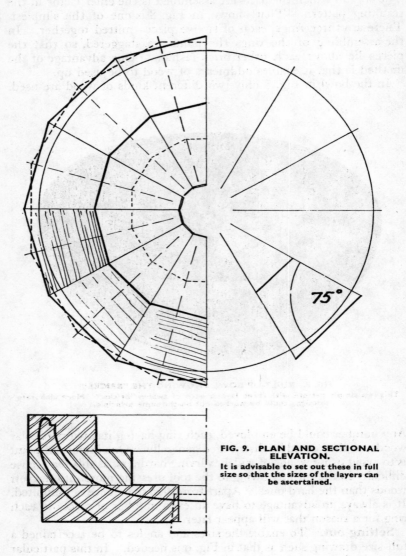

FIG. 9. PLAN AND SECTIONAL ELEVATION.
It is advisable to set out these in full size so that the sizes of the layers can be ascertained.

generous in this, because it is difficult to centre the bowl exactly and a little latitude is a safeguard.

Cutting the blocks. Assuming that you are using twelve blocks per ring the ends of all pieces will be cut off at 75°. If you have a circular saw the cutting is simple. It is merely a matter of setting the mitre gauge to the required angle and cutting one end of all the pieces. A stop is then attached to the table, the wood pressed up to

FIG. 10. THE GLUED-UP ASSEMBLY READY FOR TURNING.
Each layer is glued up independently and the surfaces levelled. All three are then put together.

it, and the cut made. If you are making a number of bowls, and are using strip material, you have only to reverse the wood after each cut, press it up to the stop, and repeat the process. The angle is the same, of course. If a fairly small-toothed saw is used, or if a planer saw is used, the parts can be glued up without further attention, though it is obviously necessary for the angle to be accurately set.

In the case of handwork a mitre box will have to be used, this having kerfs specially sawn in it at the required angle. When strip material is being used one end of all the strips is sawn first. A piece of wood with one end sawn to the required angle to form a stop is nailed to the bottom of the box as in Fig. 11 (A). The wood is held up to this and a cut made at the kerf. After removing the required block the strip is turned over, pushed up to the stop, and the process

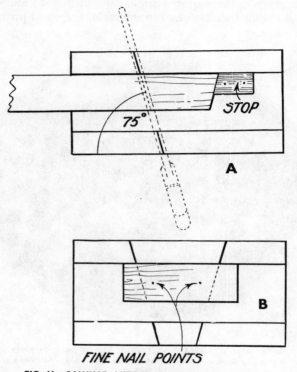

FIG. 11. SAWING MITRES OF BLOCKS BY HAND.
For strip mitreing follow method (A). When small oddments
are being used follow method (B).

repeated. In this way a single kerf in the box enables all the cuts to be made.

When oddments of wood are used all the pieces are brought to the same width first, and the method at (B), Fig. 11, followed. The kerfs are positioned so that their distance apart gives the required length. When the parts for the lower ring of the bowl (which are shorter) are being sawn a parallel packing piece can be placed at the back of the box. If the wood shows any tendency to move, a couple of nails can be partly driven into the bottom of the box, nipped off short, and the projections filed to a sharp point.

For a really good job the ends of the pieces should be trimmed on the mitre shooting board as in Fig. 12. Little more than a single shaving is needed.

Assembling. Each ring is glued up independently on a flat board with paper beneath to prevent it from sticking. The parts are rubbed together, and the simplest way is to assemble each ring

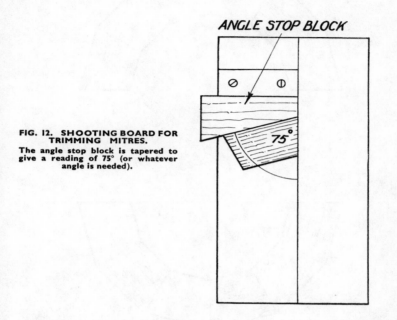

ANGLE STOP BLOCK

FIG. 12. SHOOTING BOARD FOR TRIMMING MITRES.
The angle stop block is tapered to give a reading of 75° (or whatever angle is needed).

in two halves. When the glue has set, each half ring is placed on the shooting board and the joints trimmed as in Fig. 13. Since the rear of the plane bears on the other end of the half ring the joint is bound to be true. This is much simpler than attempting to glue the whole in one operation, since it is always awkward to trim and insert the last piece. The slightest inaccuracy in the mitres can throw the whole thing out. This is the reason why an even number of pieces is an advantage.

When all three rings are together the surfaces are trued up with the plane and glued together, cramps being used. To prevent the parts from floating out of position on the wet glue a few positioning nails can be tapped in as in Fig. 14.   Fig. 10 shows the completed assembly.

Turning.   The outside is turned first, and the work can be mounted on the face plate and held with screws as at (A), Fig. 15. The bulk of the waste can be removed with a small gouge, but scrap-

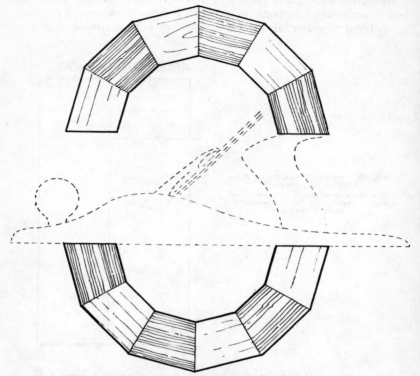

FIG. 13.   HOW LAYERS ARE ASSEMBLED IN HALVES.
This enables the last mitres to be trimmed easily with the plane.

ing tools ground from old files are needed to finish off.   Since one half of each block will be turned against the grain a fine cut is essential for finishing.   Most woods can be scraped with the tool straight from the grinding wheel.   The burr set up when the edge is ground helps the cut.   Other woods may need the finer edge given by oil-stoning; in other cases it is an advantage to actually turn up an edge much as a cabinet scraper is sharpened.   Turn the whole thing to shape, then go over again taking fine cuts only.

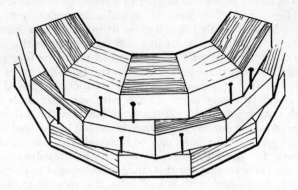

FIG. 14. NAILS USED TO POSITION LAYERS WHEN ASSEMBLING.

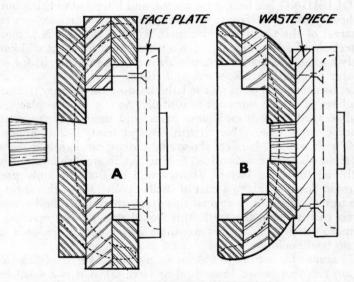

FIG. 15. TWO STAGES IN TURNING.
The outside is turned first and a bottom plug inserted as at (A). To complete the inside turn a recess in a waste piece to take the base as at (B).

The hole at the bottom is turned to a regular circle and is slightly tapered (Fig. 15, A). A block is turned independently to fit it and glued in. Make sure that it is a close fit inside as it is here that the joint shows. Level this when dry and remove from the face plate.

To turn the inside a waste piece is attached to the face plate with screws and a recess turned in it to take the bottom rim of the bowl as in Fig. 15 (B). It is glued in with newspaper interposed to enable it to be removed easily later. Turn with scraping tools as before and finish with glasspaper. If the lathe has reversible drive it is an advantage in taking out any slight roughness left by the tool in working against the grain. The bowl can be finished with the special french polish made for the lathe applied whilst work revolves slowly. A certain knack is necessary for this since it is essential to know when to stop. It is burnished with saliva from the mouth applied with a pad. Alternatively wax polish can be used. A useful compromise is to lightly body the bowl with french polish and finish with wax.

CHAPTER 14 : POLISHING

POLISHING is a beauty treatment, and intended to bring out the beauty *already there*; to enhance the grain so that we can enjoy a marvel of the Creator as shown in wood. It is needed, too, for protection, to encase the object in a transparent film that will handle nicely and also to seal the grain against changes in the air, for wood is liable to swell, shrink, warp, and so on.

Let us consider a bowl on the lathe needing this beauty treatment. You have of course turned it beautifully, no ribs or sore places, and hand scraped those troublesome parts, and used glasspaper to get a nice clean surface. Now (with boys at least) beauty treatment starts with water. It raises the grain, and we can lightly glasspaper it afterwards or use a hand scraper to get it smooth again (use a scrubbing brush on boys). It may well be that this only presses the grain down again, so a coat of shellac polish to set the fibres will help to make them firm against this glasspapering or hand scraping. If you wish to stain the work, this would rather upset matters, but for more instructions in this consult *Staining and Polishing*, a companion handbook.

My aim so far is to have a clean open-grained surface (if the wood has any) so that boiled linseed oil or olive oil, if it is a salad bowl, can penetrate. You can use furniture creams or beeswax and turpentine, for the purpose is to give "life" to the wood and to seal the grain too. Some woods are so close-grained that this does not happen; box, for instance, may well be left alone, with just a coat of polish for clean handling.

French polish. I'm old fashioned and like ordinary french polish afterwards or for a final coat to seal in what we have used first. You must not run the lathe too long, or too fast, as it will burn the surface and cause ribs of dirty polish which will need to be cleaned off. The heat generated will also force the first coats to go further into the grain, and give the work a hungry look.

It may well be you would like a filled surface. A light papering after you have put the first coat of oil, or wax on, will do that for the dust forms a filler. There are several friction polishes on the market, and we used one at the works for cheap jobs. You just brush it on, and when nearly dry hold a cloth on rather firmly to burnish it as the work revolves.

Wax. Carnauba wax is one that can be obtained in various coloured chunks from dark brown to light. At one handicraft exhibition I saw some lovely turned work finished off in this alone, but I did wonder if the glossy surface would stand up well to use. It is a very hard wax, and when you cut it with a knife it fractures rather like a stone. My opinion is that used sparingly on hard close-grained wood it gives a marvellous finish, but if put on too thick would chip off. So it does seem that something to soften it is desirable, and is probably the trade secret of some of the polishes we can buy. Beeswax takes a lot of beating, and I put the paste inside a cloth and hold it onto the revolving work. This does not waste much, and the heat generated helps to force it into the grain It can leave the surface a bit grubby but a light use of shellac polish would alter that.

Cellulose. So far I have not mentioned cellulose, although at one time I used twenty-five gallons a week. Handles were dipped into a tank of it and withdrawn in five minutes or so by a young lady. The job was to turn a handle one revolution in five minutes and this lifted a board with handles hanging down from the tank. Now this is all mentioned because some jobs can be dipped into a container and withdrawn, but the trouble is that the outside surface forms a skin and the liquid slips down underneath forming lumps, but it is a process used for some turned work.

I have seen cellulose used too most successfully on elm bowls. You just brush plenty on of clear cellulose, and then at the right moment run the lathe at a medium speed. You hold a cloth on

(continued on page 149)